The letters of James, Peter, and Jude number among the most neglected parts of the New Testament. The authors of this study argue that the letters in question are more theologically significant than is often considered the case, and have a distinctive role to play in contemporary discussion of Christian faith. Andrew Chester sets James in context and discusses its main themes: eschatology, faith and works, ethical and social teaching; and (to a lesser extent), law, wisdom, human nature, ministry, God, and Christ. He addresses the problems that James has been seen to pose, in relation to Paul, for the canon and coherence of the New Testament, and points to the significance of James for the present day, especially in its attack on the rich and powerful and its demands for faith to be lived out in everyday life. Ralph P. Martin in turn shows how Jude and 1 and 2 Peter give insight into Jewish Christianity in its earliest development; how the Christian movement was understood in an outlying region of the empire; and how the post-apostolic church utilized the memory of Peter for its practical needs. The resulting picture constitutes an expert and long-overdue treatment of these letters as valuable theological documents in their own right.

NEW TESTAMENT THEOLOGY

General Editor: James D. G. Dunn,
Lightfoot Professor of Divinity, University of Durham

The theology of the letters of James, Peter, and Jude

This series provides a programmatic survey of the individual writings of the New Testament. It aims to remedy the deficiency of available published material, which has tended to concentrate on historical, textual, grammatical, and literary issues at the expense of the theology, or to lose distinctive emphases of individual writings in systematised studies of 'The Theology of Paul' and the like. New Testament specialists here write at greater length than is usually possible in the introductions to commentaries or as part of other New Testament theologies, and explore the theological themes and issues of their chosen books without being tied to a commentary format, or to a thematic structure drawn from elsewhere. When complete, the series will cover all the New Testament writings, and will thus provide an attractive, and timely, range of texts around which courses can be developed.

THE THEOLOGY OF THE LETTERS OF JAMES, PETER, AND JUDE

ANDREW CHESTER

Lecturer in Divinity, University of Cambridge

RALPH P. MARTIN

Professor of Biblical Studies, University of Sheffield

CAMBRIDGE
UNIVERSITY PRESS

Published by the Press Syndicate of the University of Cambridge
The Pitt Building, Trumpington Street, Cambridge CB2 1RP
40 West 20th Street, New York, NY 10011–4211, USA
10 Stamford Road, Oakleigh, Melbourne 3166, Australia

First published 1994

Printed in Great Britain at the University Press, Cambridge

A catalogue record for this book is available from the British Library

Library of Congress cataloguing in publication data
Chester, Andrew.
The theology of the letters of James, Peter, and Jude / Andrew Chester, Ralph P.
Martin.
p. cm. – (New Testament Theology)
Includes bibliographical references.
ISBN 0 521 35631 8 (hardback) – ISBN 0 521 35659 8 (paperback)
1. Bible. NT. Catholic Epistles – Criticism, interpretation, etc.
I. Martin, Ralph P. II. Title. III. Series.
BS2777.C44   1944
227′.906 – dc10   93–33910
CIP

ISBN 0 521 35631 8 hardback
ISBN 0 521 35659 8 paperback

Contents

Editor's preface

Although the New Testament is usually taught within Departments or Schools or Faculties of Theology/Divinity/Religion, theological study of the individual New Testament writings is often minimal or at best patchy. The reasons for this are not hard to discern.

For one thing, the traditional style of studying a New Testament document is by means of straight exegesis, often verse by verse. Theological concerns jostle with interesting historical, textual, grammatical and literary issues, often at the cost of the theological. Such exegesis is usually very time-consuming, so that only one or two key writings can be treated in any depth within a crowded three-year syllabus.

For another, there is a marked lack of suitable textbooks round which courses could be developed. Commentaries are likely to lose theological comment within a mass of other detail in the same way as exegetical lectures. The section on the theology of a document in the Introduction to a commentary is often very brief and may do little more than pick out elements within the writing under a sequence of headings drawn from systematic theology. Excursuses usually deal with only one or two selected topics. Likewise larger works on New Testament Theology usually treat Paul's letters as a whole and, having devoted the great bulk of their space to Jesus, Paul, and John, can spare only a few pages for others.

In consequence, there is little incentive on the part of teacher or student to engage with a particular New Testament document, and students have to be content with a general overview, at best complemented by in-depth study of (parts of) two or three New Testament writings. A serious corollary to this is the degree to which students are thereby incapacitated in the task of integrating their New Testament study with the rest of their Theology or Religion courses, since often they are capable only of drawing on the general overview or on a sequence of particular verses treated atomistically. The growing importance of a literary-critical approach to individual documents simply highlights the present deficiencies even more. Having been given little experience in handling individual New Testament writings as such at a theological level, most students are very ill-prepared to develop a properly integrated literary and theological response to particular texts. Ordinands too need more help than they currently receive from textbooks, so that their preaching from particular passages may be better informed theologically.

There is need therefore for a series to bridge the gap between too brief an introduction and too full a commentary where theological discussion is lost among too many other concerns. It is our aim to provide such a series. That is, a series where New Testament specialists are able to write at a greater length on the theology of individual writings than is usually possible in the introductions to commentaries or as part of New Testament Theologies, and to explore the theological themes and issues of these writings without being tied to a commentary format or to a thematic structure provided from elsewhere. The volumes seek both to describe each document's theology, and to engage theologically with it, noting also its canonical context and any specific influence it may have had on the history of Christian faith and life. They are directed at those who already have one or two years of full-time New Testament and theological study behind them.

University of Durham   JAMES D. G. DUNN

Abbreviations

ANRW	Aufstieg und Niedergang der römischen Welt
b.	Babylonian Talmud
BAGD	Bauer, *A Greek-English Lexicon of the New Testament*, ed. W. F. Arndt, F. W. Gingrich and F. W. Danker
Bib	*Biblica*
BHT	Beiträge zur historischen Theologie
BTB	*Biblical Theology Bulletin*
CD	The Damascus Document (From the Cairo Genizah)
Cath	*Catholica*
CBQ	*Catholic Biblical Quarterly*
CNT	Commentaire du Nouveau Testament
EKK	Evangelisch-Katholischer Kommentar zum Neuen Testament
ET	English translation
EvT	*Evangelische Theologie*
EvQ	*Evangelical Quarterly*
ExpTim	*Expository Times*
HNT	Handbuch zum Neuen Testament
HTR	*Harvard Theological Review*
Interp	*Interpretation*
JBL	*Journal of Biblical Literature*
JETS	*Journal of the Evangelical Theological Society*
JSNT	*Journal for the Study of the New Testament*
JR	*Journal of Religion*
JSNTSS	Journal for the Study of the New Testament Supplement Series

KD	*Kerygma und Dogma*
LingBibl	*Linguistica Biblica*
MeyerK	Meyer, *Kritisch-exegetischer Kommentar über das Neue Testament*
NovT	*Novum Testamentum*
NovTSuppl	Supplements to *Novum Testamentum*
NRSV	New Revised Standard Version of the Bible
NTS	*New Testament Studies*
IQS	The Community Rule (from Cave 1 at Qumran)
RTP	*Revue de théologie et de philosophie*
SB	Sources bibliques
SBLDS	Society of Biblical Literature Dissertation Series
ST	*Studia theologica*
ThR	*Theologische Rundschau*
ThV	*Theologische Versuche*
TZ	*Theologische Zeitschrift*
WBC	Word Biblical Commentary
WUNT	Wissenschaftliche Untersuchungen zum Neuen Testament
ZNW	*Zeitschrift für die neutestamentliche Wissenschaft*
ZTK	*Zeitschrift für Theologie und Kirche*

I

The Theology of James

ANDREW CHESTER

Introduction

James presents a unique problem within the New Testament. The questions that loom over it are whether it has any theology at all, and whether it should have any place in Christian scripture. Issues of this sort have haunted James for most of its history. So for, example, it was only relatively late on and with considerable reservation that it was included in the canon.[1] The agenda for the modern discussion of James has been set above all by Martin Luther, who famously described James as an 'epistle of straw'. He held that it had no place in the New Testament, since it says nothing about Christ, or his death and resurrection, and contradicts Paul and the true gospel of justification by faith by preaching justification by works.[2]

Luther's polemical attitude to James has been enormously influential, especially (although by no means exclusively) in Protestant scholarship. As a result, James has been left on the margins of the canon and formulations of Christian doctrine, and is rarely given any place at all within an overall theology of the New Testament.[3] Within the present century, however, it is probably the classic commentary of Martin Dibelius that has

---

[1] James was only accepted as canonical at the end of the fourth century, and our earliest clear evidence for it being seen as 'scriptural' comes from Origen in the third century. This may well be due not only to doubts about its apostolic authorship, but also to its anti-Pauline stance or more general apparent lack of distinctive Christian themes. See further Dibelius-Greeven 1976. 5–54.

[2] Luther does also speak more positively in places of James, but his verdict is overwhelmingly negative, and he sees its poor theology as the reason why it was not accepted as canonical; see further Dibelius-Greeven 1976, 54–6.

[3] As Luck 1984, 2, notes, James is for example mentioned only briefly and disparagingly in Bultmann's *Theology of the New Testament*, and not at all in Conzelmann's *Outline of the Theology of the New Testament*.

exercised more influence than anything else on the study of James, and, although Dibelius stands in the German, Lutheran tradition, he differs from Luther in important respects. He sees James as consisting of general paraenesis (or exhortation), with isolated wisdom material connected only by catchwords and lacking any overall argument or coherence; hence also it has no theology at all (Dibelius-Greeven 1976, 1–11, 21–34).

Although this brief summary of Dibelius' position may suggest a disparaging attitude towards James, he is in many respects very positive, and serves as a healthy corrective to · Luther. For example, he makes sense of James as essentially a work of popular piety, which belongs to the ordinary people and their religion (Dibelius-Greeven 1976, 38–50). At the same time, however, Dibelius obviously leaves us with the problem of whether we can understand James theologically, and if so, how. That is, Dibelius and Luther between them seem to leave us with the choice of saying that James either has no theology or else that he deliberately presents a wrong, perverse theology. It is in some ways difficult to say which of these is worse; Luther's position is the more stridently polemical, but Dibelius, in the end, also represents an effective indictment of James theologically.

If I found Luther or Dibelius completely convincing, I would not have undertaken to write on James for this series. However, James has much more to offer than is often thought, and more of specifically theological significance than, for example, Dibelius allows. Admittedly the importance of James, theologically, should not be exaggerated; but, equally, James can be shown to have a distinctive role to play in contemporary discussion and formulation of Christian faith. This does not mean that we can treat James as though the work of Luther, Dibelius, and others did not exist. On the contrary, it is important to engage with these issues and the discussion arising from them, just as it is equally important not to be constrained by them. Hence the question of what kind of writing James is, and the context in which it was written, will be taken up in ch. 1; that of its theological content and distinctiveness in ch. 2; the problem of James' relation to Paul, and the problems it is perceived to create for the whole question of the canon and the inner consistency and coherence of the New Testament, in ch. 3; and the issue of the continuing significance of James, both positively and negatively, in ch. 4. But, anticipating this discussion, I want to assert at this point that James is worth taking seriously, and its theological significance specifically worth searching out.

CHAPTER I

James: background and context

The questions involved here are complex and disputed. James is an enigmatic and puzzling work. It is brief and apparently disjointed, and easily gives the impression of jumping haphazardly from one topic to another.[1] James also fails to fit into any of the main theological traditions or trajectories of early Christianity, and the question is inevitably raised of whether it is distinctively Christian at all.[2] Yet in fact there are several interesting points of contact with early Jewish and Christian tradition, both positively and negatively, not least with Paul.

1.1 RELATION TO EARLIER TRADITION

1.1.1 Paul

The relationship of James to Paul is of crucial importance for questions of the date and setting of the letter, and also for evaluating James theologically. The discussion here above all concerns 2. 14–26. With its highly positive assessment of works, its attack on justification by faith, and the way it uses the paradigm of Abraham and Gen. 15. 6, it appears to stand in a very negative relation with what Paul says, especially in Gal. 3–4 and Rom. 3–4. It is also much more plausible that James is familiar with Pauline teaching and practice, than that Paul is responding to James (see ch. 3). But, although James is prob-

---

[1] So e.g. Dibelius-Greeven 1976, 5–7.
[2] A. Meyer, *Das Rätsel des Jakobusbriefes*, Giessen 1930, presents in fullest form (following earlier writers such as Spitta and Massebieau) the thesis that James represents an originally Jewish work, lightly Christianized.

ably opposing a distinctively Pauline position, it is not clear that this is done from knowledge of Paul's own writings; and, apart from 2. 14–26, there is not a great deal of evidence of contact with Pauline tradition.[3] The nature and implications of the relationship between 2. 14–26 and Paul are of central importance for the history and contemporary interpretation of James, and are taken up more fully in chs. 2 and 3.

1.1.2 Jesus' Teaching

More positively, there are striking connections between a considerable amount of the material contained in James and the teaching of Jesus as it appears in the Synoptic Gospels. For example:

Has not God chosen those who are poor in the world to be rich in faith and heirs of the kingdom which he has promised to those who love him? (Jas. 2. 5)

Blessed are the poor in spirit, for theirs is the kingdom of heaven [cf. 5.5: 'Blessed are the meek, for they shall inherit the earth']. (Matt. 5. 3)

So also the polemic against the rich in 5. 1 can be compared with the Woe of Luke 6. 24 (cf. 6. 25), and the prohibition against using oaths and the demand to say simply 'yes' or 'no', in 5. 12, is close to Matt. 5. 34. The points of contact are mainly with the Sermon on the Mount in Matthew (or Sermon on the Plain in Luke), but they extend to other parts of Matthew and Luke, as well as some sayings in Mark.[4] The nature of the parallels, however, makes it highly improbable that James has used either Matthew or Luke.[5] The arguments that James has used the sayings–source Q are not particularly convincing either. Hartin (1991, 140–217, 220–44) asserts that James used the Q tradition as it was being developed within

---

[3] Mayor 1913, xci–cii provides a full list of possible (including unlikely) parallels.

[4] *Ibid.*, lxxv–lxxxviii again provides the fullest list of parallels; cf. also Hartin 1991 140–98.

[5] Amongst others, M. H. Shepherd, 'The Epistle of James and the Gospel of Matthew', *JBL* 75 (1956) 40–51, argues for James as dependent on a knowledge of Matthew, but the case is unconvincing; cf. e.g. Davies 1964, 403–4.

the Matthaean community (a source designated Q^{Mt}), but well before the composition of the gospel; that is, James was familiar with the original Q and also Q^{Mt}, but not with the final redaction of Matthew. However, although Hartin is convincing in noting the affinities with the sayings-tradition in Matthew, his attempts to tie this down more precisely in terms of the Q tradition are question-begging. Even the most obvious similarities in wording between James and the gospels are not particularly precise; often they are quite general or even remote. At least some can be explained by James using common Jewish tradition. Again, although there are striking similarities with Matthew, both for Jesus' teaching and more generally, there are impressive links with Luke as well. For example, Davids argues that in a number of ways James is closer to Luke's version of the Sermon than to that of Matthew.[6] This raises obvious problems for Hartin's thesis. To speak of James using Q in written form begs questions, still more so with the further refinements Q^{Mt} and Q^{Lk} (the Q tradition as it was being developed within the Lucan community), implying *written* tradition. We are inevitably brought back to the fact that the verbal parallels are often not at all close.[7] For much of the material, James is most probably making use of a tradition of Jesus' teaching, which will have at least general affinities with 'Q'; but it is quite possible, for example, that James is drawing on sayings in Aramaic form. We need, therefore, to be much more careful than Hartin about which precise tradition of teaching James is using. Finally, it is striking that, while James obviously draws on early tradition of Jesus' teaching, it does so without any of this teaching being attributed to Jesus.

1.1.3 Wisdom traditions

There is clear evidence in James of the influence of wisdom tradition. 4.6 quotes Prov. 3. 34, while there is obvious affinity

---

[6] Davids 1982, 47–50; but he is concerned to stress that James has used the unwritten Jesus tradition freely, and not Matthew or Luke.

[7] Davies 1964, 403 rightly points out (in contrast to Hartin) that the parallels between James and Q are very few.

with wisdom traditions in, for example, 1. 19 (cf. Sir. 5. 11; Prov. 10. 19; 17. 27), 1. 26 (Ps. 39. 1) and 1. 27 (Sir. 4. 10; 7. 35; Job 31. 16–21).[8] There are many further allusions and verbal parallels to Wisdom literature (especially Sirach, but also Job, Proverbs, Psalms, and Wisdom of Solomon) in all five chapters of James. More important than this, however, is the fact that much of James belongs to the style of teaching of the Wisdom literature.[9] This represents an intellectual tradition developed over several centuries, especially concerned with understanding and insight. But this is not an abstract concern; it is directed sharply towards practical advice and instruction to enable the reader to know what to do in various situations, and how to follow the right path and avoid the way of folly. Much of the advice is general (although not abstract) in nature, but it is all based on seeking wisdom, or being given it, as prerequisite. So James shows dependence on this tradition, in emphasizing the need to seek true wisdom from God (1. 5) and to show its effect in the whole of life (3. 13–18, and throughout), and the practical advice and instruction that is associated with this throughout the letter.

One specific theme which is prominent in the Jewish wisdom tradition (although by no means restricted to it) is that of the suffering of the innocent, righteous individual.[10] It is given its most clear and sustained treatment in the book of Job, which calls in question much of previous wisdom tradition and more general Jewish theodicy by showing a righteous, innocent individual not being rewarded by God, but suffering terribly. This theme is also prominent in a number of Psalms and in the wisdom tradition otherwise, and is taken up above all in Wis. 2–5 (cf. also Sir. 2. 1–11). All this is important background for James, not only, obviously, for 5. 11, with specific reference to Job, but also more widely, both in 5. 6, 10 and in the whole theme of the oppression of the poor. Already in the Psalms, and

---

[8] Cf. also e.g. 3. 2 (Qoh 7. 20; Sir. 14. 1); 3. 3 (Ps. 32. 9); 3. 6 (Sir. 8. 3; Prov. 16. 27; Ps. 120. 2–4); 3. 8 (Ps. 140. 3; Sir. 38. 17–21); 4. 13–14 (Prov. 27. 1; Ps. 102 3; Job 7. 7; Wis. 2. 4).

[9] Martin 1988, lxxxvii–xciii gives a brief and helpful summary of the main issues; a more detailed treatment is provided by e.g. Hoppe 1977 and Luck 1984, 10–30.

[10] See further Martin 1988, xciii–cxviii.

certainly in the Wisdom of Solomon and Sirach, a close connection is made between the innocent who suffer and the poor
who are oppressed.

The wisdom tradition thus impregnates James throughout,
although it is question-begging simply to describe James as a
'wisdom document', without qualification.[11] It is still more
misleading to claim that James takes up the developed tradition of personified (or hypostatized) wisdom.[12] James does in
many ways have the characteristics of a wisdom writing, but it
is important to realize, for a proper understanding of James'
concerns and theology, that it uses wisdom traditions and
material creatively. For example, the wisdom tradition is
modified through the influence of James' eschatological perspective. This is akin to a phenomenon we encounter in Jewish
texts, especially the Enoch tradition and other apocalyptic
writings. In the case of James, however, the distinctive feature
is that it draws especially on the central thrust of Jesus' proclamation of the kingdom.[13] Hence James uses wisdom tradition
as one of several perspectives, and it is very important background for its form and content. But James is not controlled by
it, and, especially for its theology, it is not all-important.

1.1.4 Other texts and traditions[14]

There are some notable points of contact between James and
1 Peter. For example, 1. 1 (1 Pet. 1. 1); 1. 2–3 (1. 6–7); 1. 21

---

[11] Hoppe 1977 and Luck 1984 both overemphasize the importance of wisdom theology
for the theological argument in James, but Luck rightly follows Schlatter 1927, 418,
against Dibelius-Greeven 1976, in stressing that James is not an amorphous collection of wisdom teaching, but is thematically ordered, with logical connections.
Nevertheless, Popkes 1986, 149–51, properly stresses, against Luck and others, that
James does not simply take over wisdom tradition passively, but uses it in a
mediated and creative way.

[12] As e.g. Hartin 1991, 94–7 does; see further under section 2.9 below.

[13] Baasland 1982 qualifies his description of James as '*the* New Testament wisdom
document' by noting its novel emphasis on eschatology (although he fails to note the
Jewish parallels for this). He also holds that all the important themes in James are
found in the Synoptic tradition, and above all that what separates James from the
wisdom tradition binds him to Jesus; thus the wisdom sayings in the Synoptics
appear in a new light through the proclamation of the kingdom of God.

[14] For parallels between James and these texts, and discussion of their significance, see
e.g. Mayor 1913, lxxxviii–xci, cii–cviii; cf. Schlatter 1932, 67–77.

(1. 23, 2. 1–2); 4. 6–7 (5. 5–6). It is not simply a question of verbal parallels, however, but of common themes and concerns. Equally, it is hardly plausible that James has used 1 Peter or is dependent on it; it is much more probable that 1 Peter is familiar with James, if either is dependent on the other. Both, however, may be drawing independently on a common tradition. Again, Jude may (on the basis of its opening and one or two further references) be familiar with James, but in any case James does not draw on Jude at all. There are interesting points of contact with parts of the Johannine literature, but these probably reflect common tradition, not dependency of one on the other. Finally, the Didache and *Hermas* have clear links with James, and may be drawing on it.

1.2. AUTHOR, DATE, AND SETTING

The task of setting James more precisely in context is difficult. As far as author and addressees are concerned, it would appear that 1. 1 gives clear information, but on closer examination it is tantalizingly ambiguous. There is general agreement that the author could only introduce himself simply as 'James' if he were a well-known figure in the early Christian movement. Of the five named 'James' in the New Testament, James the brother of Jesus is the only really plausible candidate.[15] If so, however, it is strange that nothing is said about Jesus that reflects personal knowledge of him. It is also the case that the theological concerns that emerge from the letter do not fit well with Gal. 2, where James appears to have a hard-line position on observance of the law, especially concerning food and circumcision. In fact it is by no means impossible that the James of 1. 1 is one we know nothing at all of otherwise. Similarly, 'to the twelve tribes of the Diaspora' most naturally suggests that the letter was written to Jewish-Christians outside

---

[15] This is not the place to discuss the possibilities; see further e.g. Mayor 1913, i–lxxxiv; Dibelius-Greeven 1976, 11–21; Martin 1988, xxxi–xli; Davids 1982, 2–22. If the identification with James the brother of Jesus is correct, it could of course be either an authentic self-designation or a pseudonymous claim to James' authority and prestige; this issue is clearly bound up with that of the dating.

Palestine, but strong arguments have been put forward to take
it to refer to Jewish-Christians within Palestine, or Jewish and
and Gentile communities (or even the whole church) outside
Palestine.

From the points of contact between James and Jewish and
early Christian tradition, and the sparse information provided
by 1. 1, sharply contrasting arguments have been put forward
to explain the nature and context of James.[16] Probably the
most widely held view is that which sees James as a pseudonymous work, dating from AD 80 or later, addressed to communities outside Palestine and attacking a developed or perverted
form of Paulinism. A particularly interesting representative of
this position is Popkes, who emphasizes the importance of
setting the theological problems in the context of ecclesiological and social reality.[17] He argues that the two main problems,
of wealth and poverty, and of proving faith in life, show that
those addressed most plausibly belong to the sphere of the later
Pauline mission church, where communities have tendencies
towards individualizing, dualism, and spiritualizing. The
majority of those addressed belong to the ambitious, upwardly
mobile middle class, set in the cities. Similarly James is not
essentially a social reformer, but takes a moral position,
opposing not wealth and power as such, but their abuse, and
advocating social help and good deeds.

Popkes' argument, however, is not without problems. The
portrayal of the Pauline communities as upwardly mobile
middle class, and the author himself as a high-minded middle-
class social reformer, probably owes more to the situation of
Popkes as a modern Western interpreter than to the situation of
first-century Christianity. The widely accepted idea that early
Christianity had a substantial minority of well-off influential

---

[16] On the question of dating, Davids 1982, 4 provides a very useful table summarizing
the different views, with further discussion in the following pages.

[17] Popkes 1986, 53–91, taking up the stimulating argument of J. B. Souček, 'Zu den
Probleme des Jakobusbriefes', *EvT* 18 (1958), 460–8. Heiligenthal 1983, 26
(cf. 2–7) also sees Christianity having to adapt to the changed historical-
sociological situation of the Hellenistic cultural world outside Palestine; hence the
new communities were open to anyone and had no fixed structures at the start.

members[18] is certainly open to criticism. Along with these problems concerning the socio-economic situation, Popkes also has to overinterpret 2. 14–26 and other texts, and play down too much the Jewish character of much of James.

This last point is important. The sheer Jewishness of James is striking. Hence the view that James is an originally Jewish writing, subsequently Christianized (see note 2, above), or, more commonly, that it is authentically by James, written from within Palestine to a community in Palestine.[19] The socio-economic situation in this case is seen as that where large landowners oppress and exploit poor landowners, tenant farmers, and day-labourers, and rich merchants increase their profits at the expense of the poor. On this view, James is taking the side of the poor Christians (the Jerusalem community or more widely) against the rich in the increasingly bitter conflict in first-century Palestine.[20] The most specific evidence for James as a Palestinian work is the fact that the reference to the climate fits only Palestine and a small further area of the eastern Mediterranean otherwise.[21] But, if it is held that James predates AD 48 and any controversy with Paul (see ch. 3), there are obvious problems, as also with the reference to 'the twelve tribes of the diaspora' in 1.1.[22] More, plausible is a position that sees James written in the fifties to Jewish-Christians outside Palestine.[23] This would allow sense to be made of 2. 14–26; and, if the letter was sent to a community in Antioch, the arguments concerning socio-economic conditions and climate would hold more or less as for Palestine. It might seem

---

[18] This position is represented by e.g. E. A. Judge, *The Social Pattern of Christian Groups in the First Century*, London 1960; G. Theissen, *The Social Setting of Pauline Christianity*, Edinburgh 1982; W. A. Meeks, *The First Urban Christians*, New Haven 1983.

[19] So e.g. Adamson 1976; 1989, 53–86; Maynard-Reid 1987, 8–11.

[20] Maynard-Reid 1987 gives an impressive interpretation of James on this basis; cf. also Adamson 1989, 228–58.

[21] That is, the reference in 5. 7 to 'early' and 'latter' rain would really fit only Palestine and Syria; cf. e.g. Davids 1982, 183–4.

[22] It is possible, but far from convincing, to take the reference to the Diaspora to be to that of the 'dispersion' (Acts 8. 1) of the early Jerusalem community throughout Palestine; Davids 1982, 17–18 indicates the plausibility of this interpretation, but (64) takes it to refer more obviously to a Diaspora outside Palestine.

[23] So e.g. Mussner 1981, 11.

strange in this case that nothing was said about circumcision and food-laws, but these issues could be seen as already belonging in the past.

This reconstruction has difficulties of its own. It is true that the good Hellenistic Greek of James can no longer be held to be decisive proof that the letter was not written by the brother of Jesus.[24] Nevertheless, the Greek style still needs some explaining, and in other respects as well the case for James' authorship of this letter as a whole is not compelling. Hence the attraction of the argument that the tradition-history of James is more complex, and consists of the basic core of the letter, authentically by James, with editing and development of it at a later stage.[25] This position is in some ways problematic as well, but has the merit not least of being compatible with the fact that much of the evidence in James is open to widely differing interpretation. That is, the socio-economic evidence fits first-century Palestine, but the same basic conditions existed throughout the Roman Empire. Nor does the apparently primitive and underdeveloped theology, especially Christology, and lack of developed hierarchy and organization, demand an early date: James belongs essentially within Jewish Christianity,[26] and could well represent a form of the messianic sect unaffected, internally, by Pauline and other developments. On the other hand, although 2. 14–26 especially suggests reaction to a perversion of Paul, and may be a generation or more on from the apostle, it need not be so; the scenario of

---

[24] Thus e.g. Hengel 1987, 251, who in his work otherwise has done more than anyone to show that the traditional division between 'Jewish' and 'Hellenistic' categories in general is untenable, sees it as perfectly possible that James could in Jerusalem have had a secretary well-educated in Greek rhetoric, and by no means impossible that James himself could have received a good grounding in Greek education in his native Galilee. The best and fullest discussion of James' style and language is provided by Mayor 1913, ccvi–cclxviii.

[25] So Davids 1982, 2–22 argues that James is a two-stage work, containing a great deal of material which is early and may well come from James himself, but brought into its present form by a later redaction, either by James himself or a member of his church, in the period *c.* 55–65 or 75–85. Martin 1988, lxix–lxxvii argues that the letter contains a deposit of James' teaching that was taken to Antioch by his disciples, and edited and adapted there to meet the needs of a community in Syria.

[26] Cf. e.g. L. Goppelt, *New Testament Theology*, vol. 2, Grand Rapids 1982, 208–11.

James taking issue with Paul on the basis of reports received is quite plausible.

Finally, then, there can be no certainty at all; nor is it possible here to discuss the problems more fully. But, as a basis to work from, it seems to me most probable that James is representative of a specific form of Jewish Christianity, and is addressed to a particular group or groups of Jewish-Christians outside Palestine, perhaps most plausibly in Antioch. As such, it draws on Jewish traditions of wisdom, especially, eschatology and prophecy, as well as early tradition of Jesus' teaching, and uses these to aid in its pastoral concern and urgent call to the community it addresses to change its way of life.[27] It stands in conflict with Paul, whether in contemporary debate or at some distance in time removed. Despite the speculative nature of much of this, it may help us understand the nature and context of James, and allow us to gain perspectives on why James' theology and message take the particular form, and include the specific themes, they do.

---

[27] The urgent hortatory tone of James is evident from the fact that 54 out of a total of 108 verses are imperative; this, and the pastoral concerns of James are emphasized by e.g. Popkes 1986, 126–8, 207–10. So also W. H. Wuellner, 'Der Jakobusbrief im Licht der Rhetorik und Textpragmatik', *LingBibl* 43 (1978), 5–66, stresses the importance of analysing James from the perspective of the way it would have made an impact on its readers.

CHAPTER 2

James: theology

The division of this chapter into separate themes is for convenience and clarity. It undoubtedly reflects present-day theological concerns more than those of James as such. The intention is not to suggest that James has a sustained overall (still less, a systematic) theology, but simply to do some justice in the short space available here to the main theological emphases of the work.

2.1 ESCHATOLOGY

It is sometimes said that James, even if it has some theology worth discussing, has no real eschatology. For example, Popkes holds that eschatological themes are found only in the outer framework of James (1. 1–18; 5. 9–20), and not in the main central section, where the heart of the message lies. So also Lohse plays down the supposed eschatological emphasis; there is, he argues, very little, and it is only one minor theme among many.[1]

These arguments, however, are suspect. Obviously the eschatological emphasis of James should not be exaggerated, but it certainly has significance out of proportion to its direct and explicit usage.[2] Equally, the fact that explicit eschatological

---

[1] Popkes 1986, 44–45; Lohse 1957, 12–13. Popkes rejects arguments that the 'inner core' of James contains eschatological material; but Burchard 1980a, 28–31; 1980b, 317, 325 rightly notes that the eschatological perspective in James belongs not only to the outer framework, but also to the central section of the letter (e.g. 2. 5, 12–13). The fact that the end is near serves as a spur to patience and perseverance, and to the issues of faith, works, and the law.

[2] Baasland 1982, 122, 124 argues that James sees everything from the perspective of judgement (cf. also ch. 1, note 13); so also Blondel 1979, 144, Bieder 1949, 108–10, Burchard 1980a, 28–31, 1980b, 317, 325, Obermüller 1972, 235, 238, 241, 243 all stress the central importance of eschatology for the letter and its theology as a whole.

themes are found primarily in the outer framework of the letter, does not (*pace* Popkes) necessarily diminish their significance. This argument can obviously be turned round; that is, the substantial 'introductory' section can be seen as outlining the main, important themes for the central section of the book, where they are taken up both implicitly and explicitly, and are resumed in the concluding section. The themes set out at the start provide an important perspective for the whole work.[3]

Thus 1. 2–4, set emphatically at the very start of the letter, introduces the theme of trials or testing. This theme belongs, in the framework of Jewish eschatology, to the final tribulation which will usher in the messianic age and final rule of God.[4] Hence, paradoxically, the writer can call on those he addresses to rejoice at the prospect of tribulation, because what awaits them in the end is the positive reward and fulfilment of the final age. This point is made clear by 1. 12–13, which speaks of God giving the 'crown of life' (the eschatological reward) to those who endure the trial.

The most explicitly eschatological section in James is 5. 7–8(/9), where the main theme is *the imminent coming of the Lord*. The writer sees the eschatological denouement as near at hand, although it is not completely clear what form he thinks that this will take; most probably it is the parousia, the return of Christ, but it may be the coming of God himself, to bring in the new age and final judgement. As often in the New Testament (and the Jewish eschatological tradition that underlies this), the promise of the coming of the Lord is double-edged, involving reward for endurance in the final trial, but also the threat of judgement; the latter is directed here specifically not against the wicked, but against those in the community who attempt to usurp for themselves the divine role of judging.

Judgement is itself one of the eschatological themes that can be found, at least implicitly, in the 'central' section of the letter, as, for example, 2. 12–13; 4. 11–12. The latter, again, warns

---

[3] Baasland 1982, 122 rightly notes that the opening section (1. 1–18) contains all the main themes of the letter.

[4] See further D. Allison, *The End of the Ages has come*, Philadelphia 1985, esp. 5–25.

against judging others, and in addition emphasizes the urgent, life-and-death issues that the final judgement involves. In 2. 12–13, this final judgement is also interestingly set in terms of, and against, the law. At the same time, although 2. 13 enunciates the principle (familiar otherwise within Judaism) that God's mercy outweighs his justice in judgement, the same passage makes very clear that judgement will be according to conduct; more precisely, according to works of mercy, or the lack of them.[5] So also 4. 9–10 may have a similar eschatological dimension, with the prophetic indictment of 4. 9, and the threat of destruction and promise of final reward. This may govern not only the immediately following 4. 11–12, but also the preceding 4. (6/)7–8, related in turn to 4. 1–4, and the theme that false action and denial of God lead to judgement and destruction. Hence also the stress here on the urgent need to be clean and humble.

The clearest example in James of an eschatological indictment on the pattern of the Old Testament prophetic tradition is to be found in 5. 1–6. Here we have a savage denunciation, reminiscent of the eighth-century prophets (especially Isaiah, Micah, and Amos),[6] of false action, lack of mercy and exploitation of the poor and helpless. All this inevitably leads to destruction, implicitly on the day of the Lord (cf. 5. 3), while the passage as a whole represents an exultant anticipation of the disaster that is to come soon (5. 1), or has in part already arrived (5. 2–3), for the rich. There are further references to judgement and condemnation in James, more casual and less developed than 5. 1–6, but probably still implicitly eschatological. This is the case, for example, at 5. 12, while this theme of judgement is also set in 3. 1 at the start of the long section on speaking and teaching, where it is invoked as a threat that looms over those who abuse their position. It can also be argued that the stress on the transient nature of wealth in 1. 9–11 and 4. 13–15 gains added sharpness from the implicit reference to the imminent end and final judgement.

[5] This theme is also familiar within Judaism from as early as Sir. 27. 30–28. 7; Tobit 4. 9–11.
[6] E.g. Isa. 3. 11–15; 5. 8–10, 23; 9. 18–10. 4; Amos 2. 6–7; 5. 11–12; 8. 4–6; Mic. 2. 1–5.

In 1. 12 by contrast, the positive theme of *blessing* is invoked for the one who comes through the eschatological testing. That is, the beatitude form is used in order to express the promise of divine, eschatological reward. This is comparable at least in general terms to the Beatitudes in Jesus' teaching, where the blessings are related to the kingdom and new age. Strikingly also (just as in Matt 5. 3, 5) it is specifically the kingdom that is made the eschatological reward and inheritance for the poor. This gives a very sharp focus to the discussion, within 2. 1–13, of partiality, oppression, and the treatment of the poor and oppressed. Conversely, 4. 9 recalls the Lucan Woes on the rich and unjust, which form the antithesis to the shorter Lucan form of the Beatitudes, and have clear eschatological emphasis on judgement. This theme, and especially 2. 5 with its reference to the kingdom, may help shed light on 2. 8, within its immediate context. In particular, the phrase *nomos basilikos*, usually rendered 'royal law' (or something similar), is probably to be understood not as giving the law an elevated or superlative status in itself, but, much more plausibly, as the law 'concerning the king' or 'relating to the kingdom'.[7] That is, for James, the love command can epitomize the law (see section 2.4), as it relates to the new messianic age, the age of the kingdom, and as it is to be lived in anticipation of this.

Further, 1. 25 makes the beatitude form apply precisely to those who keep the 'law of freedom', to which 2. 12 assigns an eschatological connotation. 1. 25 also denotes the law as 'perfect', and perfection is for James an *eschatological* theme, as is shown, for example, by 1. 2–4, where it is the result of (or reward for?) withstanding the final tribulation; it is also an important theme otherwise for James. Finally here, 3. 17–18 may also deliberately evoke the Beatitudes or related tradition (especially, for example, Matt. 5. 9) by linking those who make

---

[7] This is variously taken to be the real significance of the phrase by e.g. W. F. Arndt and F. W. Gingrich, *A Greek-English Lexicon of the New Testament and other Early Christian Literature*, Chicago 1957, 138; Jeremias 1954–5, 370; Johnson 1982, 400–1 (who relates it closely to Jesus' proclamation of the kingdom, and the mention of the kingdom in 2.5); Weiss 1976, 110; Blondel 1979, 149; Adamson 1989, 281–5; Davies 1964, 405.

peace directly with the, implicitly, eschatological reward of righteousness.[8]

Not all of the passages in James discussed here are explicitly eschatological, but individually and cumulatively they show the importance of this perspective for James. The themes of judgement, testing, and threat are set over, and within, the work as a whole, but so also are those of hope for the messianic age and final reward, and the immediate, urgent implications of this for the way life should be lived in the present.

2.2 FAITH AND WORKS

Discussion of the relation between faith and works in James usually centres on 2. 14–26. Outside of specialist studies of James, this is very often the only section referred to. This is hardly surprising, in view of the sharply formulated character of this section and the overall history of the interpretation of James. Nevertheless, it needs to be noted that this section does not suddenly appear out of nowhere in the letter. The themes that are prominent, indeed notorious, in it have already been introduced and discussed earlier in the letter, especially 1. 19–26; 2. 1–13[9] (cf. also 1. 2–4, 5–9), and are taken up subsequently (if less directly) in 3. 13–18, 4. 11–12 (cf. 4. 13–17). The main point that runs consistently through these sections, and is emphasized throughout, is the absolute necessity for the way of life of those addressed to correspond to their profession of faith. James insists that if what is claimed is not borne out by what is done, in very specific and practical ways, the so-called 'faith' is false, and merely a hollow shell. Hence all these sections of the letter are set consistently and relentlessly against any discrepancy between word and deed, faith and works, and ruthlessly expose false claims and false living.

It is precisely here that James' eschatological dimension

---

[8] This theme is closely linked in Matthew with both perfection and the kingdom, in the Beatitudes and elsewhere. (For 1. 25, cf. possibly Matt. 5. 48, where perfection is connected, implicitly, with the law and the messianic age.)

[9] This point is made by e.g. Heiligenthal 1983, 27–33; Burchard 1980a, especially 27–30, argues for 2. 14–26 to be understood above all in the context of 2. 1–13.

shows its cutting-edge. That is, the whole issue is set sharply in terms of the final judgement (2. 12–13). Those who fail to live out love for their neighbour (for James the epitome of the law and the profession of faith: 2. 1, 8!) will come under divine judgement and stand condemned, without any hope of God's mercy. For James, it is only those who show mercy who will receive mercy, only those who show compassion in everyday, practical ways who can stand before God and be accepted by him in the last judgement (2. 21, 24; and perhaps 1. 25 as well).

It is important to take some account of what James says in the other passages before considering 2. 14–26. The first main theme that emerges, especially in 1.19–26 and 3. 12–18, is that of *hearing and doing*. In 1. 19–26 James emphasizes the importance of hearing the divine word, which is set over against potentially harmful human speech and human perversity in general. This is then developed further into the central theme of the section, the need not only to hear but above all to act. The spur to action, and the norm for what is required, are provided by the law of freedom, itself characterized (2. 8, 12) by the love command. Here the contrast between false, self-deceiving human religiosity and true religion and regard for God is vividly drawn. The latter, for James, must be made manifest in specific acts of mercy for the poor and oppressed.[10] In 3. 13–18, the point is that those who are truly wise show this by their works and whole way of life. This way of life, governed by divine wisdom, is characterized by humility, unselfishness, and related virtues, and has its eschatological reward. All this is set in contrast to falsely claimed human wisdom, that expresses itself in harmful talk and action. So also, finally, 4. 11–12 again sets harmful speech, especially in the sense of passing judgement on others, in contrast to doing (or fulfilling) the law, and as coming under condemnation in the final judgement.

---

[10] Blondel 1979 rightly says of 1. 26–27 that faith for James cannot be individual piety, but must show itself in the service of the brethren. The way James specifies what is required is familiar from Jewish tradition; e.g. Sir. 4. 10 (more fully developed, in later sources, as an *imitatio Dei* theme: e.g. Pentateuchal Targums, except Onkelos, at Gen. 35. 1; b. Sota 14a; Gen. Rab. 8. 13).

The second main issue is that of *partiality and observing the law*. This is the central concern of 2. 1–13; so 2. 1–7 scathingly exposes the implications of sycophantic respect for the rich, powerful oppressors and the correlative process of humiliating the poor and oppressed. This for James contradicts claims to faith, and negates the nature of the kingdom; it is God's kingdom, and belongs to those whom he has called. Correspondingly, 2. 8–13 uncompromisingly emphasizes that to fulfil the law and be acceptable to God (implicitly in the final judgement) means specifically to love one's neighbour and to perform acts of mercy (cf. also 1. 27). The issue is set in harsh and rigorous terms: to fail to fulfil the law at any point (and partiality is precisely an example of such failing) is to be guilty of all of it and to be condemned (cf. Gal. 3; Matt. 5. 19–20). Thus final judgement is invoked on failure to fulfil the law and practise consistently the faith that is professed. Favouritism and faith are irreconcilable.

In 2. 14–26 the overriding theme is that faith without works is dead and useless. This recurs as a constant, hammer-like refrain throughout the section (2. 17, 20, 26). It is illustrated first (14–17) by an example very close to that in 2. 1–7; that is, the discrepancy between the faith that is claimed and the action which fails to correspond to it. In this case, however (as distinct from 2. 1–7), the incident belongs entirely within the community, and concerns the discrepancy between saying the right thing and failing to do it. But the really striking point (as with 2. 1–13) is that the argument is immediately focused in a very specific way, and demands practical expression of love and mercy. It is therefore in no sense an abstract discussion of faith and works. The next stage of the argument is notoriously obscure and difficult,[11] but the main point is clear: James insists that faith and works are completely inseparable, and it makes no sense to speak of 'faith' as though it can exist on its

---

[11] The problem is constituted above all by the first few words of v. 18, where the objection 'You have faith and I have works' seems to be the wrong way round. It is tempting to reverse this to produce better sense in the immediate and wider context. Martin 1988, 86–8 gives a useful review of the main attempts to resolve the difficulties and references to further discussion, which I cannot go into here.

own. Thus a bland confession of monotheism has nothing distinctive or effective about it. The argument is supported by using developed Jewish tradition of Abraham, and the Aqedah motif, thus interpreting one scriptural passage (Gen. 15. 6) by means of another (Gen. 22).[12] The main point of using scripture in this way is that Abraham's 'faith', which Gen. 15. 6 speaks of ('believed in'), and which allowed him to be accepted by God ('was reckoned to him for righteousness'), is in no sense abstract. Abraham's trust in God (his 'faith') is made manifest, in the most striking way, by his willingness to sacrifice his only son. It is his works, exemplified by this specific action, that gives substance to his faith and allows him to be accepted. Hence it is not faith on its own, but only faith along with works (specifically, that is, completed or made perfect by works) that gives Abraham any standing before God. The argument of this section as a whole is that the same applies to those whom James addresses. This point is then reinforced from the example of Rahab.

From this discussion of 2. 14–26 in relation to the other relevant passages, some main theological perspectives for James emerge:

(1) *works are primary*,[13] at least in the sense that they are essential for justification, that is, for being accepted, and not condemned, by God in the last judgement. Works are the only way of proving that a person has faith, true religion, and divine wisdom. So also, works are the only way of showing that a person fulfils the law fully, in the sense of the new law of

---

[12] I. Jacob, 'The Midrashic Background for James II, 21–23', *NTS* 22 (1975), 457–64, argues that James' interpretation here is close to what we find in 1 Macc. 2. 52 and Sir. 44. 20–1. On the developed traditions of Gen. 22 and the Aqedah (Binding) of Isaac, see e.g. G. Vermes, *Scripture and Tradition in Judaism*, Leiden 1961, 193–227; S. Spiegel, *The Last Trial*, New York 1967; and specifically for the New Testament, J. Swetnam, *Jesus and Isaac*, Rome 1981. R. B. Ward, 'The Works of Abraham: James 2:14–26', *HTR* 61 (1968), 283–90, argues that James' point here is that Abraham (as also Rahab) was justified on the basis of works in the specific sense of hospitality; but Burchard 1980a, 42–3 is right to see the argument here as wider in scope than that.

[13] So e.g. Via 1969, 256; R. Walker, 'Allein aus Werken. Zur Auslegung von Jakobus 2, 14–26', *ZTK* 61 (1964) 155–92. By contrast, Heiligenthal 1983, 28 argues that 1. 2–4 show that works are derivative of faith.

freedom, which can be characterized specifically as loving one's neighbour. This point is vital for the whole understanding of works in James; that is, it is in no sense an abstract concept, but denotes above all acts of mercy and practical help for the poor and oppressed. This understanding of works belongs fully to the idea of fulfilling the law, as love for one's fellow-being, and is also completely consistent with the way of life that belongs to, and anticipates, the messianic age and divine kingdom.

(2) *faith is secondary*, at least in the sense that any claim to have faith in itself counts for nothing and provides no way of being accepted in the last judgement. At the same time, however, faith is necessary, in the sense of being presupposed by, and belonging integrally together with works. In this limited sense, faith can be seen as primary in James, even though works remains much the more important of the two. For example, in what is said about doing and hearing in 1. 22–3, doing is given primary place and importance, but obviously hearing is presupposed and indispensable. So, analogously, faith is the basis out of which works come, and in *this* sense at least works can be viewed as derivative of faith. To this extent, therefore, and in this restricted sense, there is less of a contrast or antithesis between faith and works than may at first seem to be the case, especially in 2. 14–26. But, equally, it is important that this point should not be exaggerated. It has been argued that in the discussion of Abraham in 2. 20–24, faith is the main theme, and the assessment of it is essentially positive;[14] but the central point of this section is that faith on its own is worthless, and only works can make it worth anything. So, again, the conclusion to 2. 14–26, with its analogy of the body and spirit, shows clearly that the latter (that is, works) is the more vital, and is to be seen as superior. Consequently, the positive understanding of faith in James, as far as it exists, is very much constrained and qualified. Thus faith can be infer-

---

[14] J. G. Lodge, 'James and Paul at Cross-Purposes? James 2, 22', *Bib* 62 (1981) 195–213, argues that the chiastic structure of 2, 21–4 shows faith to be primary at least in this section. Blondel 1979, 143 rightly insists that faith and works simply cannot be separated for James.

red from works, but not vice-versa. That is, James demands that faith, if it is to have any validity, must be real faith, which means that works (above all, the showing of mercy and love) must be an integral, indeed the decisive, part of any claim to faith.

(3) *faith is used in at least two different ways*[15] in the letter, as is clear from the above discussion and from a detailed investigation of the relevant passages in the letter. It is used positively, in the sense of 'true' faith, in 1. 3, 6; 2. 1, 5; 5. 15, and also negatively, in the sense of 'claimed', that is, *false*, faith, in 2. 14–26. This distinction appears complicated by the fact that 2. 14–26 has something of an 'overlap' of usage. Thus 2. 22 twice uses faith in the sense of genuine faith, on the part of Abraham. In fact, however, this passage helps to clarify the point at issue. Thus 2. 24, 26, along with 2. 22, show that 'faith' can only be properly what it claims to be when, as in the case of Abraham, it is *shown* by 'works'. That is, proper action in Abraham's case *demonstrates* his complete *trust* in God.

This brings us to the real point of the distinction and to what is at issue here. That is, 'faith' in 1. 3 denotes complete trust in God and absolute commitment to him, which survives the ultimate eschatological testing and is shown to be true precisely by this. The sense of complete trust is similar in 1. 6; 5. 15, both in relation to prayer. The remarkable expression we find at 2. 5, 'Has not God chosen those who are poor in the world to be rich in faith and heirs of the kingdom which he has promised to those who love him?' is probably also closely related to 1. 3; that is, James portrays the poor as having complete trust in God and therefore, implicitly, being able to withstand the final testing and to take their place in the new age of the kingdom. The sense of 2. 1 ('My brethren, show no partiality as you hold the faith of our Lord Jesus Christ, the Lord of glory') is less clear, but most plausibly the idea is that it is faith in Christ, and full commitment to him, that is the distinctive mark of the Christian community, and that the true nature of this faith

---

[15] So e.g. Bruce 1952; Jeremias 1954–5, although Popkes 1986, 203 wants to hold both closely together.

must be demonstrated by the way those who profess it treat others. It must not be allowed to be damaged or endangered by false living. This would serve to confirm the picture of 2. 18–19 (cf. 2. 24, 26), that a mere, minimal credal confession of faith is inadequate. It is only full, absolute trust in God, demonstrated in life and in action, as with Abraham and as in the final testing, that should truly be designated 'faith'. To make this contrast between 'true' and 'false' faith certainly goes beyond the actual terminology James uses, but fits his usage elsewhere. In 1. 26–7 he makes a straight contrast between true ('pure') and false ('vain', 'supposed') religion, while 3. 13–18 draws a clear distinction between true and false, divine and human wisdom. This is quite consistent with the way that James speaks of someone *saying* they have faith in 2. 14, whereas outside 2. 14–26 'faith' is used without qualification.

A number of issues are raised here. First, the main positive significance is placed throughout on works, which has primary place for James. It is therefore essential, for a proper under-standing of James, to develop an adequate account of what precisely he means by works, especially in its intensely practi-cal sense, and why it is so important to him.

Secondly, the question is raised of the extent to which James' treatment of faith and works, especially in 2. 14–26, is coloured by the context. In particular, it appears probable that James does not choose to introduce the topic of faith, at least as far as 2. 14–26 is concerned; instead, he finds the issue forced on him, as one that he has to deal with and redefine (Popkes 1986, 202). This assumes that James is responding to Paul's gospel of justification by faith, or at any rate a perversion of this, where 'faith' is hollow and false, and allows any kind of conduct. This polemical, constrained context would then also help to explain the negative emphasis here on faith, and the discrepancy both within this section and with what James says otherwise. As I have noted, outside 2. 14–26 James has a positive understand-ing of faith, above all in the sense of trust or commitment, and it is certainly plausible that it is this sense that is part of what he argues for in 2. 20–4. That is, Abraham shows, in Gen. 22 and his 'works' more generally, this absolute trust in God, and steadfastness. This is then set as the potentially positive corrective to the polemical strictures on false faith in the rest of the section. So true faith is faith that lasts in testing, and that expresses itself in action and in deeds of love and mercy. We have, then, a clear suggestion of positive understanding of faith by James. Nevertheless, it has to be said again that James does not independently choose to introduce faith, and he does not set out any real theology of it either. He has to take it up, and he deliberately devalues it. It is true that James demands perfection (as far as being steadfast is concerned) for faith, as for works, and sees faith as integrally and inextricably bound up with works and inseparable from them. In spite of claims that are often made, however, this does not mean that James consequently sees faith and works as being equal.[16] If he were setting out his understanding of faith in different circumstances, without having to counter a false view of faith, it is possible that he would do so. But, as the argument stands, faith, even in its positive sense of absolute trust, remains inferior to works for James.

This leads, thirdly, to the question of justification. Again, in the polemical context of 2. 14–26, James asserts that justification is by works. The negative point is that faith alone cannot save, and although faith in a positive sense is obviously involved with works, James here allows only works a positive role in justification. It can be argued that for 2. 14–26 (and especially 20–4) it makes no sense to ask whether justification is by faith or works, since the two are inextricably bound up together. But the fact remains that in this section James does not have a consistently positive or developed enough view of faith to allow for any conclusion except that works are central and indispensable for justification. It is clearly the case that James' understanding of faith is not that of Paul (that is, as a shorthand for acceptance of the salvation that God has brought about through the death and resurrection of Christ), but something much narrower. So also the understanding of justification can be seen to differ; Paul sees this primarily as the

---

[16] This claim is made by, amongst others, Lohse 1957, 4–5.

point of entry into the community, where faith is involved as
the response to God's gracious act, whereas for James it is a
question of being accepted by God at the last judgement. Here
claims to bland faith are vain, and only righteous deeds and
acts of mercy count. All this, however, raises the larger issue of
the relationship of James to Paul. The main discussion of this
question comes in ch. 3, and the only point that needs to be
made here is that there is too much special pleading often
involved in trying to make James conform to Paul. In fact, he
stubbornly refuses to.

2.3 ETHICS

In one sense, almost the whole of James can be seen to be
concerned with ethics.[17] It is here that setting James within the
wisdom tradition is at its most persuasive and helpful. Like
Jewish wisdom writings, James has a sustained collection of
instruction on a variety of topics (see section 1.1.3). It is here as
well that we might feel most sympathy not only with Dibelius'
influential interpretation of James as paraenesis, but also with
his characterization of it as loose and unconnected material.
But this does not do justice to James as a whole, and it is
important to remember that discussion of the various ethical
themes in James belongs within the wider context of the work
and its theology as a whole.

2.3.1 Control of speech

Misuse of speech constitutes a major problem, as far as James
perceives it, for those to whom he is writing. It is often difficult
to know precisely what issue the writer is addressing. Some of
the material is probably stereotyped, deriving from the
common stock of Jewish wisdom and ethical traditions, and

---

[17] See W. Schrage, *The Ethics of the New Testament*, Edinburgh 1988, 281: 'No other
New Testament document is as dominated by ethical questions as the Epistle of
James'. Cf. Heiligenthal 1983, 26; so also Blondel 1979, 141 sees James as belonging
to primitive Christian paraenesis and everyday ethics for the faithful, representing a
call to the practice of the faith.

some of what it says is deliberately general or exaggerated, or both. Yet the relative prominence of this theme, in a short letter, coupled with the specific nature of at least some of the material, suggests that the writer knows of problems that need to be dealt with.

One of the central problems concerns *teachers*, as the main passage on the use of the tongue (3. 1–12) shows clearly. But the issue is not, as elsewhere in the New Testament (for example, 1 Corinthians and the Johannine Epistles) that of false teaching.[18] Rather it appears to be arrogance (cf. also 4. 13–17), anger, and the criticizing and insulting of others in the community, directly or otherwise. Part of the problem in James may be close to that hinted at in Matthew (for example, 23. 7–8; cf. 10. 24–5), where to be a teacher, or rabbi, carries with it a sense of superiority (as in Judaism more generally). This would certainly make sense of the strong impression we get from 3. 1–12 of a situation where consider- able numbers within the community want to become teachers. It would also explain James' strong warning against this, and the space he gives to spelling out the responsibilities and dangers inherent in the role of teacher. Although 3. 1–2 obvi- ously concerns teachers, the rest of 3. 1–12 is more general. James warns against the damage that the tongue can do, and, although this is expressed in exaggerated terms, it points to real problems of strife and division caused by malicious and critical talk. This is potentially divisive and destructive; the correlative is the warning in 3. 15 about evil conduct that causes strife and schism. Hence James also issues a strong warning against gross discrepancy in the use of the tongue: it is used, in the context of worship, to praise God, but it is also used, in gatherings of the community, to utter formulas of cursing. These curses probably come in the course of argu- ments in the community, and thus contribute further to the problems. This context may also make best sense of 5. 12, with

---

[18] By contrast, Popkes 1986, 106–11 sees James as concerned with false teaching, in the wider context of this problem towards the end of the first century, but Burchard 1980b, 318–19 rightly stresses that the problem is not false teaching, but controver- sial disputes within the community.

its demand not for oaths, but for speaking plainly what is true.[19]

In the same way, 1. 19–26 confirms the impression given by 3. 1–12 that there is a prevalent tendency amongst those addressed to be too ready to speak, especially critically and in anger. 1. 19–21 may be concerned primarily with the problem of teachers who set themselves up too readily to speak, but the section as a whole is intended to apply more widely. 4. 11–12 and 5. 9 also deal with malicious slander within the community; here it is specifically set under final judgement, as is the case in 3. 1 for teachers and, implicitly, others. Again, more widely, 4. 13–17 (cf. 3. 14–16) attack harmful speech in the form of boastful, arrogant talk. Hence James advocates restraint and holding back from speaking, above all in the interests of community harmony and unity, and to counter discord. In 3. 1–12 and these other sections we see the heart of James' concerns, including what he sees as the most important ethical issues. That is, to speak evil against one's fellow and to fail to live according to what one says are equally a denial of true Christian life, fatally self-deceiving and incurring final divine judgement.

2.3.2 Suffering, testing, and perfection

In looking at eschatological perspectives in James, we have noted the importance of the theme of testing, and have seen that one main aspect of this is the context of final tribulation (1. 2–4, 12–15; 5. 7–12).[20] James uses various traditions to develop this ethical teaching, especially the example of the righteous, innocent one who suffers (see section 1.1.3). This is particularly clear in 5. 6, where the climax of the savage indictment of the rich is 'You have condemned, you have killed the righteous

---

[19] 5. 12, as much else in James, derives from early traditions of Jesus' teaching, but this does not preclude it from being used with specific ethical application in the letter.

[20] Adamson 1989, 308–16 sees the theme of testing as eschatologically orientated, and the simple and clear eschatology of James as integrally linked with ethics. J. Thomas, 'Anfechtung und Vorfreude', *KD* 14 (1968), 183–206, argues that James develops eschatologically the idea of anticipated affliction and, especially, joy from Ps. 126.

man; he does not resist you'. The phraseology is very strong and specific, and the verse could be taken to refer to a particular individual,[21] but, especially in the context of 5. 1–6, the most probable reference is to the poor, ordinary members of the community, those who have been 'killed' or 'judically murdered' by oppression or exploitation, and not allowed the basic means of subsistence. This theme is taken further: 5. 11 uses the example of Job, the prime figure in Jewish-Christian tradition of the righteous, innocent one who suffers, is tested, and is ultimately vindicated by God, while 5. 10 brings in the tradition of the suffering of the prophets. In 5. 7–11 as a whole, James is probably urging the poor, ordinary people (already brought into the picture in 5. 1–6) to be patient in the face of oppression, and so gain their final reward. James draws on an underlying Jewish tradition not only of the unjust suffering of the righteous, but also of the oppression of the poor.[22] This helps inform our understanding of ch. 1 (especially 1. 3–4, 12–13). That is, the ordinary members of the community experience suffering both in the final tribulation (still awaited), and also through oppression. They are both poor and innocent, and are urged to endure, since they cannot actually resist; so they will receive their final, divine reward, as the Beatitude allusion of 5. 11 (cf. 1. 25; 2. 5) indicates. However, James is referring not simply to the final tribulation, but to mundane everyday temptation as well. These two kinds of testing (final tribulation and everyday temptation) should not, therefore, be thought of as completely distinct from each other. They belong together in some other instances as well, for example, in the case of the temptation to compromise faith and seek riches (1. 6–8, 9–11; cf. 2. 1ff.). Both are also involved in the temptation to blame God for troubles that come, and to do evil because of one's own desires (1. 12–15).

All of this demands constant vigilance, and the virtues James advocates for being able to withstand testing and resist

---

[21] Both Jesus and James have been suggested, but no convincing arguments have been produced.

[22] See further e.g. Davids 1982, 41–7, on these themes brought together in Jewish tradition.

temptation are steadfastness, endurance, and patience. It is the nurture and practise of these that allows the individual to be 'perfect'.[23] This point is made at the very start of the letter, probably with a play on words: if they allow steadfastness to have its 'perfect work' or 'full working-out' or 'manifestation' (*teleion ergon*), they will themselves be 'perfect' (*teleioi*). This in turn can obviously be closely related to the 'crown of life' that is said in this list to be the reward that God gives for endurance. Thus persevering is associated with the 'perfect law' in 1.15, and fulfilling this law is associated with eschatological blessing. So again, picking up the connection with work (*ergon*), in 2.22 (as we have seen) Abraham's faith is said to have been made perfect, or complete, by works. Further, the one who is perfect keeps control of what she or he says. In one real sense, James offers a counsel of perfection. It does not derive only or primarily from the wisdom ideal; much more, James sets perfection as a dimension of the eschatological context of the individual and community. It belongs to the fulfilment of the law of the messianic kingdom, the love command (2. 8–10; cf. 2. 5), withstanding the testing of the final age (1. 2–4), and showing itself in acts that correspond to the law of love (2. 22). It is a demand that no one can fulfil, an impossible ideal, as James himself admits (3. 2). But that ideal of perfection is something that belongs to the eschatological, or interim messianic, age.

2.3.3 Rich and poor

The most striking theme in the whole letter is the denunciation of the rich and powerful, and corresponding concern for the poor and oppressed. Some of what is said here has close affinities with the wisdom tradition, but that is not the main point of reference, and these sections are in no sense stereotyped. It stands much closer to the prophetic tradition, and wider Jewish traditions of concern and provision for the poor.[24]

---

[23] Adamson 1989, 321–3 emphasizes the importance of the theme of perfection in James, in its ethical and eschatological dimensions; so also e.g. Luck 1984, 11–13.

[24] So e.g. Exod. 22. 21–7; Lev. 25. 35–55; Deut. 10. 16–19; 15. 7–11; cf. also note 6 above, and e.g. Davids 1982, 41–7; Martin 1988, lxxxiv–lxxxvi.

Again, these various traditions should be seen as mutually complementary, not contradictory. The affinities with the prophetic tradition are most evident in the vehement denunciation of social injustice, oppression and exploitation, above all in the direct attack on the rich landowners in 5. 1–6, although this is by no means an isolated example.[25] The immediately preceding attack on rich traders and merchants (4. 13–17) is integrally connected (cf. also 4. 1–12), and the same point is sharply evident also in 2. 6–7, even though this section is dealing mainly with the issue of favouritism within the community, and is not addressed directly to the poor. James, in these sections, exposes ruthlessly the sources of power, the nature of power relationships and the causes of conflict, oppression, and social unjustice. To live for personal gain and to exploit the poor and defenceless is the epitome of evil, above all because it is set in direct contradiction to what God requires (2. 5). Yet at the same time James insists that it is not simply the direct exploitation and oppression of the poor by the rich that constitutes the problem. It is also the obsequious favouring of the rich and powerful, for the favour it is hoped they will bestow, and the contemptuous treatment of the poor, because they can offer nothing, that serves to reinforce the injustice, suffering and imbalance of power (2. 1–7). James sets these issues in eschatological perspective, above all that of final judgement. He stresses the transience and futility of wealth and self-gratification at the expense of others (1. 9–11; 4. 14–15; 5. 1–3).

It can be seen, then, that the denunciation of the rich for their exploitation and greed, as also favours done to them for the wrong reasons, is a major theme in James. The correlative to this is that God's concern is especially for the poor, and that this should therefore be the case for the community as well. The central thrust of 2. 1–7(/13) is that God has chosen the poor and that the kingdom belongs to them (primarily if not exclusively), and it is they who should receive special attention within the community. The desperate condition of the poor

---

[25] Cf. note 6 above and especially Maynard-Reid 1987.

and oppressed is known to God, and their oppression will be vindicated in the final judgement and new age (5. 4; 2. 5–13). James reaffirms a central tenet of Jewish teaching (from the Old Testament onwards) that it is the poor, oppressed, and marginalized who matter most to God, and it is they who should matter in the community (1. 27). What is striking about 1. 27 is not the particular formulation, which is familiar from Jewish tradition, but again the prominence of this theme in so short a letter: it is *this* theme that is made the definition of pure religion and worship of God. And the famous section 2. 14–26 is sharply focused, as we have seen, on the concrete issue of caring for the poor and destitute, over against false piety. In eschatological perspective, the reversal of roles for the humble poor and arrogant rich is assured (1. 9–10; cf. 4. 9–10; 5. 1–6), because that is the nature of the kingdom that God is bringing in; but, in the meanwhile, it is the task of those in the community to anticipate the messianic kingdom and treat the poor as God would.

2.3.4 Love, mercy, and humility

In 2. 13, at the end of the section on partiality, the issue of whether or not the poor and weak are treated with mercy is made the decisive factor for the final judgement. This is closely linked with 2. 8, a pivotal verse in the section, where love of neighbour is made the epitome of the law. Although these specific terms are not used, it is the showing of love and mercy that James demands in other sections dealing with the poor and oppressed (1. 27; 2. 14–17); similarly, mercy is one of the attributes that characterizes the person who is truly wise (3. 17). Conversely, it is precisely this attitude and conduct that the rich and the oppressors (and those who court their favour: 2. 1–13) fail to show. Further, the poor and oppressed are characterized as humble, the rich and powerful as arrogant and boastful (1. 9–11; 4. 15–16; cf. 4. 9–10). More generally, beyond these specific sections, James urges those he addresses to be humble, and denounces arrogance and boasting (1. 21; 3. 13–16).

2.3.5 Overall ethical perspectives

(1) James' ethical teaching is controlled by his *eschatological* perspective. Negatively, it is eschatological testing and tribulation, and the final judgement, that underlie the demands James makes on those he addresses. Positively, they are called to live and act in ways worthy of the kingdom, which can be anticipated in part, and will soon come in its fullness. It is issues of everyday life and mundane temptation that are addressed, but they also stand under this perspective. It may be possible to understand the perfectionist element in James's ethics in this light as well. That is, it belongs to the intense, interim period of final testing, before the judgement and the onset of the kingdom.

(2) James' ethics are *social and communal*: as we have seen, James emphatically reasserts a theme of Old Testament and Jewish tradition, that God favours the poor and weak against the rich who oppress them, and so correspondingly should the community. This means that they should actively be involved in helping and caring for the weakest and most vulnerable in the community, and again this demand is set under eschatological perspective. But, although James demands their involvement in mundane, menial tasks, he is not advocating conformity to the world. Precisely the opposite (2. 1–13): they should reject and challenge the normal standards and practice of the world by the way they live and the love and care they show for those who, as far as society at large is concerned, do not count.

(3) James' ethics are *based on divine precept and command*: whether or not they presuppose the gospel, they are clearly 'consequential', in the sense that James demands that their whole way of life, both individually and collectively, be lived out consistently with, and in response to, the divine word that they have received (1. 22–25; cf. 1. 21). So James' ethics and imperative style form an integral whole, and dominate the whole letter.

(4) James' ethics can be said to be *paradigmatic* or mimetic, in the sense that James in a few places gives examples to imitate. This is especially so in the case of Abraham, who serves as a

paradigm of active obedience and good works, necessary for salvation (as does Rahab in the same immediate context). Similarly, in 5. 10–11 the prophets and Job serve to illustrate steadfastness and patience. All these examples, it should be noted, are drawn from scripture (that is, the Old Testament), and, unlike Paul, James does not point to Jesus as a figure to be imitated. This paradigmatic use of the Old Testament is borne out by the reference to Elijah in 5. 17, and more generally in James, but it is a limited theme as far as the theological and ethical significance of the letter as a whole is concerned.[26]

2.4 LAW

James has a positive understanding of the law throughout, fully in keeping with Jewish views. The law is spoken of as 'perfect', a law 'of liberty', and 'royal' (or better 'concerning the king, or kingdom'). There is no hint of criticism of it; to act against one's fellow in the community is to act against the law, to malign and criticize it, and brings the offender under the final judgement of God as lawgiver. Conversely, observing the law brings divine reward and eschatological blessing (1. 22–5).

The main passage dealing with the law (2. 8–13) does, however, pose problems. 2. 8 implies that the love command of Lev. 19. 18 is the fulfilment of the law, or the essential core of it, just as Paul does in Rom. 13. 10. This is how the passage is often understood, but the position is by no means so simple.[27] Immediately in 2. 10 it is clear that, for James, the *whole* law still applies. The specific point being made here, that failure in one point of the law involves failure in all, looks very close to

---

[26] Blondel 1979, 150–1 speaks of James having a consequential, interim and social ethic. Perdue 1981, 245 argues that the paradigmatic element derives from the Hellenistic Moralist tradition, whereas Lohse 1957, 6 sees James' ethical perspective as rooted in its Jewish heritage.

[27] V. P. Furnish, *The Love Command in the New Testament*, London 1973, 177–82 gives a useful review of the usual position; his own conclusions are close to those which I set out here. Similarly Johnson 1982 argues that, for James, keeping the law of love involves observing the commandments of the Decalogue and Lev. 19. 12–18 in their entirety; Burchard 1980a, 29–30 holds that the 'law of love' is not a summary of the whole law for James, but that the *whole* of the 'law of freedom' (2. 8–13) must be kept without exception, and compares Matt. 5. 19.

what Paul says in Gal. 3. 10. Yet, for James, in contrast to Paul, this point is in no sense polemical as far as the law is concerned. That is, James' attitude remains positive; he stands much closer to the tradition represented by Matt. 5. 19, insisting that the whole law remains in force and cannot be diminished. This may sound harsh and rigorous, but for James (and Matthew), as for Judaism generally, the law is a joy and delight, not a burden. The law makes demands, and theory and practice do not always coincide, but James is not at all inconsistent in seeing the law as still in force and at the same time speaking of the 'law of freedom' (2. 12; 1. 25).[28]

The question still remains what exactly James means by using Lev. 19. 18 in 2. 8. He does not reduce the whole law to this single command; nevertheless, it is significant that it is this command that he uses. It fits not only the immediate context, where the partiality of 2. 9 is clearly a denial of love of one's neighbour, but also the whole of the dominant ethical teaching of the letter. That is, showing love and mercy in action is the essential requirement for the individual and community; so failure to observe the laws concerning adultery, murder and the other commands is incompatible with love of one's neighbour as well. Hence Lev. 19. 18 shows the focal point of James' emphasis. Yet the full law is still in force. James refers only to the ethical code (as with the decalogue here), and not the cultic. It cannot, however, simply be concluded from this that the cultic law is necessarily abandoned. The fact that nothing is said, for example, about food laws, circumcision, or the temple is not conclusive, since if James belongs to a firmly Jewish-Christian tradition, the natural assumption (unless it is specifically challenged) would be that that Jewish practice and observance of the law would continue. Hence the silence here should not be over-interpreted; the question remains open.

---

[28] Possibly the phrase echoes Jer. 31. 31–4, in ther sense that the law sets the community free in the eschatological age. Burchard 1980a, 30 sees this law of freedom as intended primarily not to regulate life, but to show how to stand in the final judgement. On the larger question of the law in Judaism, see e.g. E. Schürer, *History of the Jewish People in the Age of Jesus Christ*, rev. G. Vermes *et al.*, Edinburgh 1973–87, vol. 2, 468–87; E. P. Sanders, *Judaism: Practice and Belief, 63 BCE-66 CE*, London 1992, 190–240.

For James, the law is specifically linked to the messianic kingdom and the new age (2. 8; cf. 2. 5; see section 2.1). It is in the interim period leading up to this age that perfection in observing the Torah can be demanded. Its requirements, as summed up in Jewish tradition, are specific, concrete, and communal, as well as pointing to the nature of the messianic age. In addition, there are close links between the nature and content of the law and the themes overall of wisdom and teaching.

2.5 WISDOM

James, as well as drawing on wisdom tradition throughout, also treats wisdom as a theme in its own right, particularly in the two sections, 1. 5–8 and 3. 13–18, both of which paint an impressive picture. In 1. 5–8 wisdom is portrayed as something to be sought, and above all as a gift from God.[29] The contrast is immediately drawn (1. 6–8) between those who seek wisdom in faith, and those who, torn by doubt, do not. These themes are set in the immediate context of the final tribulation, and eschatological joy, perfection, and blessedness. In 3. 13–18, the point is made emphatically that true wisdom comes from above (3. 15), and that the necessary correlation of possessing true wisdom is to show its effects in specific actions (or works). The contrast is drawn between false and true wisdom; the former is characterized by jealousy, ambition, and boasting, which divide and destroy, while the latter is characterized by those qualities that build up the community and have a direct, observable effect in the life of the community. James here takes up the tradition that distinguishes sharply between the way of true wisdom and the way of folly.

Wisdom has also been perceived as an underlying theme in 1. 16–18 and 2. 1–13. It is not completely implausible that wisdom as a specific theme is alluded to without being mentioned, but we need to beware of claiming too much for the

---

[29] As in Jewish wisdom tradition; e.g. Prov. 2. 3–6; Wis. 7. 7; 8. 21; but, as Davids 1982, 71–2 rightly notes, the eschatological dimension of James here sets it close to e.g. 2 Bar. 44. 14; 59. 7; 1 Enoch 5. 8.

treatment of wisdom in James. This is especially the case with claims that wisdom in James is effectively equivalent to the spirit in the New Testament otherwise.[30] There are interesting parallels between 3. 17–18 and what Paul lists as the gifts of the spirit in Gal. 5. 22–3; certainly, also, wisdom and spirit are used in parallel in Jewish wisdom texts. But to speak of James as having a 'wisdom pneumatology' (Davids 1982, 56) goes well beyond the evidence. Much of the New Testament shows clearly that the spirit is a prominent and central phenomenon of early Christian experience; but there is no mention of the spirit in James. Equally, the understanding of the divine spirit is developed profoundly in Paul and John, but Prov. 8. 22–31 and related developments are not taken up in James. Thus 3. 15, 17, which speak of wisdom as 'from above', denote wisdom as being of divine or heavenly origin only in a general sense, not as part of specific (or hypostatized) developments, and not in relation to the spirit. Hence attempts to make James conform to the usage of the New Testament otherwise or to the developed pattern of Christian experience and theology should be resisted. Within Judaism, it was quite possible to speak of wisdom without implying reference to the spirit, and this is so for James. Still less is it justifiable to speak of James having a 'wisdom Christology', the case for which has to rest solely on a dubious interpretation of 2. 1 (see section 2.9).

2.6 SIN AND HUMAN NATURE

It is clear that James perceives the major problem, theo-logically, to lie with human nature and the human condition.[31] It is the divided nature of the individual that lies at the heart of all the problems that James sees in the community; above all, the failure to live out the faith that is professed, and the deep divisions within the community that result from this gulf between word and action. The double nature is, for James, bound up with desire, which lures the individual into doing

---

[30] Especially, J. A. Kirk, 'The Meaning of Wisdom in James: Examination of a Hypothesis', *NTS* 16 (1969–70), 24–38.

[31] Especially Blondel 1979, 145; Popkes 1986, 45–7, 130–1, 191–4; Eichholz 1961, 44.

evil. These concepts are closely related to the Jewish understanding of the two *yesers*, especially the evil *yeser*, or inclination, which represents the pull to evil inherent within this
fundamental division in the individual.[32] James' analysis is
built out of this Jewish concept, and is specifically focused on
desire, that always craves for more at the expense of others.
The individual is not sinful or evil as such, or the source of
wrongdoing, just as God is not the source of evil either. James
begs the question of where evil comes from; probably there is
an implicit cosmological, as well as individual, dualism, but
James may well simply be working with a traditional Jewish
understanding. He does not think through the issue logically,
to its inevitable conclusion, although in speaking of the individual's own desire he may seem to imply that it is inherent in
human nature.[33]

James' analysis is limited, and does not probe as far as asking
how human nature comes to be as it is, where the evil desire (or
inclination) derives from, or whether it could be different.
Certainly James *implies* that individuals can resist from their
own resources, but again it is not clear whether this is what he
means. In 3. 2 James, in a more mundane way, accepts that
everyone is prone to sin; however, he also offers a remedy,
focused on asking God for wisdom (1. 5; 3. 13), that manifests
itself in all that is good, not in an abstract way, but in action (3.
17–18; cf. 1. 19–21). Provided wisdom is sought in complete
trust, it will overcome the (potentially) divided human nature.
Again, James' argument begs the question of whether the
individual can help being as he is, and whether, therefore, he
should be held culpable. At least, however, he posits the ideal
of the person who observes the law, has true wisdom, and

---

[32] Marcus 1982 argues that the phrase 'his own desire' in 1. 13–14 corresponds to the
Jewish concept of the *yeser*, and that references to the effects of the *yeser* pervade
James; he finds striking parallels to James' usage in Sir. 15. 11–20 and several
Qumran texts, as well as other Jewish writings. So also O. J. F. Seitz, *JBL* 63
(1944), 131–40; *JBL* 66 (1947), 211–19; *NTS* 4 (1958), 327–34, finds the origin of
the concept of *dipsuchos* ('double-minded', a term also used in Hermas, Barnabas,
and the Didache) in the two *yesarim*, or inclinations, as evidenced especially by the
Qumran texts (and later Rabbinic writings).

[33] Marcus 1982, 608–9 argues that 4. 5 refers to a *human* spirit and implies that it is God
who is ultimately responsible for evil; but this is by no means certain.

controls his desire and potentially divided nature, and is enabled to perform acts of mercy and otherwise live a life characterized by good works. James' perspective here is again especially eschatological, with the individual standing in danger of divine judgement (3. 1), and it is especially in the light of this that James looks for the transformation of the human condition,[34] even if again it is not made clear how precisely this is effected.

2.7 MINISTRY, WORSHIP, AND ORGANIZATION

James has no developed ecclesiology. The impression given by the letter is that he neither knows nor wants any formal structure, hierarchy, or organization. He uses 'synagogue' and '*ekklesia*' apparently interchangeably; it is an undeveloped model, probably close to Jewish practice. *Elders* may be important, as they are in early Christianity otherwise, but the only role mentioned is that of healing, and there is no indication that they exercise authority or power.[35] *Teachers* are important, and implicitly have prestige and social status, but there is no indication that they belong to any structured authority within the community. All we really gather is that they exist in too great numbers and overplay their role. Nor is there any sign of spiritual authority or power; healing is the task of elders, and is not attributed to the spirit, and nothing is said of gifts of the spirit, speaking in tongues or collective experience of the spirit. The reference to prayer and singing (5. 13) may belong to the context of worship; at any rate, James sees *prayer* as important (5. 13–18; cf. 1. 6), both individually and collectively.[36] The impression given is of a 'community of the word',[37] where teachers especially are important (or at least self-important),

[34] Blondel 1979, 145; Obermüller 1972, 238; Popkes 1986, 209.
[35] Burchard 1980b, 318 sees the elders as officials, but their authority as no more than that of anyone else in the community; so also teachers are not essentially different from other community members.
[36] As Lohse 1957, 15–16 notes, prayer must be expressed in full trust to be effective, for healing and otherwise.
[37] Popkes 1986, 103–4; Burchard 1980b, 319 speaks of a 'learning community' that is concerned with the law, teaching, wisdom, and perfection.

but which is acutely threatened by a breakdown between theory and practice, between what is said and what is done. It is a community in which problems may arise, and there are brief hints in the direction of church discipline (5. 19–20),[38] but the main emphasis is on pastoral care and restoration. There is no reference at all to common meals, or the Lord's Supper or Eucharist. *Baptism* is probably alluded to (for example, 1. 18, 21), and again the focus is on the (implanted) word, but the importance of baptism here is not as great as is sometimes claimed.[39] Once more, James should not simply be made to fit the New Testament and early Christian practice otherwise.

2.8 GOD

James, like much of the New Testament, does not present a specific doctrine of God, but his understanding becomes clear enough from passing, casual allusions. What emerges belongs very much to the common belief and practice of first-century Judaism. Belief in the existence of God is simply assumed; the reference to confession of belief in one God (the Shema: 2. 19) is disparaging not because of the content, but because of the context, where the wider position involved is being attacked. So also God is portrayed as the *creator* (3. 9; 1. 17), and specifically as the Father of lights; that is, as having supreme control over the universe. 1. 17 shows in addition that he is seen as the *Father*, who is characterized by grace and giving freely. He is unchangeable (1. 17), trustworthy and good. So also he is incorruptible, having nothing to do with evil, and being able neither to tempt nor be tempted. Yet at the same time, he does not overlook evil; hence the importance of his role as eschatolo-

---

[38] For more developed forms of this, see e.g. Matt. 18. 15–20; 1 Cor. 5. 1–13; 6. 1–8; and within Judaism, e.g. 1QS 5. 25–6. 1; CD 9. 2–8.

[39] G. Brauman, 'Der theologische Hintergrund des Jakobusbriefes', *TZ* 18 (1962) 401–10 especially overstates the case, finding references to baptismal liturgy, preaching and teaching pervasively (and implausibly) in James; Luck 1984, 16–18 also exaggerates the importance of baptism for James. By contrast, Popkes 1986, 136–46 rightly argues that James takes over much early baptismal tradition, but reworks it for his own purposes, with no great interest in baptism as such.

gical judge and lawgiver. James can be seen as a theocentric writing which above all wants to portray God as merciful to the humble poor and oppressed.[40]

2.9 CHRIST

James says notoriously little about Christ; that is one of the great puzzles of his writing. There are only two explicit references (1. 1; 2. 1), and, although a little more can be gleaned from what he says briefly and in passing, it is necessary to resist attempts to argue for more than there really is. The most obvious Christological feature is the use of *kyrios* (Lord: 1. 1; 2. 1; the use of Christ is really as part of a proper name). The significance of the use of *kyrios* in James is not certain, but, since the same term is used in the letter to denote God, and it is at times not clear who is referred to, Christ or God, it represents a potentially important usage. There is also some evidence to support arguments for a 'name' Christology in James (e.g. 2.7),[41] but it is not a particularly developed or explicit theme as such. Some of the material which is adduced for 'indirect Christology' in James is interesting;[42] but to try to find anything much in the way of developed or explicit Christology is little more than special pleading. The most interesting Christological usage in James is that at 2. 1, and above all the phrase 'our Lord Jesus Christ, the Lord of Glory'. The precise interpretation of this is difficult.[43] The problem above all lies in how to interpret '*tes doxes*' (the glory), which comes as a genitive at the end of the phrase; the difficulty is not least that all the preceding words, following 'faith' (*pistis*) are genitive as well. It is very improbable that it governs faith (that is, 'glorious faith'). It could be that *tes doxes* is in apposition to the

---

[40] See further Adamson 1989, 345–63, one of the best sections in his book, and Popkes 1986, 199–202.

[41] Mussner 1970, 113.

[42] Mussner 1970, 114–16 finds in e.g. 1. 27; 2. 8; 5. 1–6 evidence for such 'indirect' or 'horizontal' Christology, showing Christ on the side of the poor and oppressed.

[43] A full discussion of possible interpretations is provided by Mayor 1913, 79–82, and Hoppe 1977, 72–8. The phrase, although difficult, should not be understood as a later Christian addition, in whole or part.

preceding genitives, that is, 'our Lord Jesus Christ, the Glory'.[44] The use of 'Glory' as an attribute of God is already clear in the Old Testament, and subsequently within Judaism, the Aramaic word for glory, *Yaqara*, is increasingly used as a way of describing or speaking of God. This may be what we have at Luke 22. 69. It would certainly be a very elevated usage, since, although it does not simply identify Jesus with the Shekinah, it would nevertheless come close to making Christ identical with God. But, although this remains a possible interpretation, the phrase as a whole is too complex and difficult for there to be any certainty that it is right; and there is no support for such an elevated Christology anywhere else in James.[45] The other main possibilities are to take *tes doxes* as defining 'Christ' (that is, 'Christ of Glory'),[46] or to take it as defining, as a genitive of quality, the phrase as a whole (that is, 'our glorious Lord Jesus Christ').[47] It is awkward in either case, but not impossible. The latter, 'our glorious Lord Jesus Christ', is preferable. The point would then be that Christ is thought to be sharing in the heavenly glory, or the glorious heavenly world.

If we could be sure what the sense of 2. 1 is, we could be more specific about James' Christology; by using the same word, *kyrios*, of Jesus as of God, and by the striking phrase at 2. 1, James hints at the way a developed Christology might emerge, but he does not draw out the implications, and certainly does not have the elevated Christology sometimes read into 2. 1 and claimed for him. Nor does he says anything about the death of Christ or its saving significance, or about the resurrection.

2.10 THEOLOGY OF JAMES: SUMMARY

James' theology is limited in many respects. He says nothing for example about the spirit, and does little more than hint at

---

[44] E.g. Mayor 1913, 80–2; Laws 1980, 95–7.

[45] Hartin 1991, 94–7, while not taking *tex doxes* in apposition, argues (on the basis of 2. 1–13 as a whole) that 2.1 denotes Jesus as the wisdom of God; his discussion is, however, confused and unconvincing.

[46] E.g. Burchard 1980b, 322; cf. 1 Cor. 2. 8.

[47] E.g. Ropes 1916, 187; Dibelius-Greeven 1976, 1–28; Mussner 1970, 116; Davids 1982, 106; Martin 1988, 60.

an understanding of other themes, such as Christ, God, baptism, worship, and organization. Nor does he develop ideas about wisdom very far, although his treatment is positive as far as it goes. So also his understanding of the law is very positive, within the limited scope of his discussion, and makes an impressive and largely original contribution within the New Testament. It is sin, the human condition, and misuse of speech that James sees as the fundamental problems that need to be addressed. These and other ethical concerns permeate the whole letter, while the eschatological context and perspective are important for these issues and in their own right for James. Above all, while James says little about faith and justification, and is mostly negative about faith, he has a highly positive, if not particularly profound, theology of works. It is this especially that shows that James' theology is rooted in the concrete, specific issues of how people live in relation to each other in everyday life.

CHAPTER 3

James and the New Testament

In many respects James is an isolated work within the New Testament as a whole, unlike anything else we find in the canon. Yet it is clearly related to other New Testament writings (see section 1.1), above all and most problematically, to Paul.

The relation of James to Paul notoriously sets up a tension within the canon. It is not the only example of this in the New Testament, but it is the most acute.[1] The problem, put simply, is whether James *can* stand alongside Paul in the New Testament canon, and whether it *should* do so.[2] These are essentially the questions put by Luther, sharply and polemically, and they have dominated the discussion of James ever since. Yet the issue goes right back to the problem of James' acceptance into the canon, and the questions it raises about its apostolic authority and relationship to Paul. At any rate, we are faced acutely with the question of whether the tension thus set up within the canon is intolerable, and whether in the light of all this the canon can have any inner coherence.

The issues that need to be addressed, as far as the theology of the New Testament and the question of the canon are concerned, are whether Paul and James contradict each other, or whether they can in any sense be seen as mutually complementary. The case for flat contradiction is substantial. It centres on

---

[1] As Eichholz 1961, 7, notes, such tensions exist within the Pauline corpus and within the Synoptics, quite apart from those that can be found between different New Testament works.

[2] Cf. Eichholz 1953, 5–6.

Jas. 2. 14–26,[3] above all 2. 24, set in contrast to Paul, for example, in Rom. 3. 28. For Paul, justification is by faith and not by works; for James, justification is by works, and cannot be by faith alone. As we have seen, James constantly reiterates the basic point: faith on its own, without works, is useless, barren and dead (2. 14, 17, 20, 26). So, for James, faith can be deduced from works, but not vice-versa, and it is works not faith that save. For Paul, by contrast, no one can be justified by works (Gal. 2. 16; Rom. 3. 20; cf. Gal. 3. 2, 10).

Faced with this apparently stark contradiction, and Luther's strictures on James, modern scholarship has adopted a variety of positions, at least some of which try to resolve the problem:[4] (1) James is seen as very early (pre-AD 48), and James and Paul do not come into contact or conflict at all;[5] (2) James is again pre-AD 48, but is replied to, or attacked by, Paul;[6] (3) James is later (fifties or early sixties) and is making a direct attack on Paul or Pauline theology;[7] (4) James is much later than Paul (within the period AD 80–120), and is attacking a perverted Paulinism, not Paul as such;[8] (5) James, whether contemporary with or later than Paul, is not really comparable with him.[9]

Clearly (1) and (5) are strategies that effectively resolve the conflict. In fact (4) and (5) are, as will be seen, for the most part, variants of each other. That is, for both, James is in essential agreement with Paul, and attacking only a perversion of Paul's gospel that Paul would himself have attacked. So only (2) and (3), along with a small part of (4), really posit a head-on conflict. There is some plausibility in all these positions (see section 1.2), and none is impossible. But (1) and (2) are the least convincing of all. Both have the merit of showing why, if the letter is authentically by James, there is no reference to the issues of circumcision and food-laws; yet for both the

---

[3] But it is worth reminding ourselves that in discussions of James, there are very sharp differences over whether 2. 14–26 is the centre of the letter or not. E.g. Lohse 1957, 3 argues for, Popkes 1986, 42–3 against.

[4] See further section 1.2, with notes 16–28 for ch. 1, above.

[5] E.g. Adamson 1989, 3–52, 195–227.

[6] E.g. D. Guthrie, *New Testament Introduction*, London 1970, 752–3.

[7] Hengel 1987; Lindemann 1979, 240–52.

[8] E.g. Popkes 1986, 53–91.   [9] E.g. Bruce 1952, 74–6.

problem is that James would have to be seen as creating the sharp antithesis between faith and works, since there is no evidence of it otherwise within first-century Judaism, while for (2) it is difficult to read Romans or Galatians as an intended reply to James. Yet (2) is right to recognise that there is a problem that cannot simply be bypassed. 2. 14–26 is not the only, or most important, part of James, but equally it is not isolated in the issues it deals with (see section 2.2). The point that confronts us is that, in the language he uses, James is almost certainly attacking a position that is central and peculiar to Paul. That is, the proclamation of the doctrine of justification by faith (alone), and the contrast between faith and works, is lacking not only in the Judaism of James, but also in early Christianity, apart from Paul and his followers.[10]

The question, therefore, is whether James is attacking Paul directly, or whether he is attacking a perversion (or misunderstanding) of the Pauline gospel. The latter position, in one or other of its versions, has been, and still is, dominant. Lohse's comment (1957, 7), that James most probably has certain Pauline slogans in view, is typical. So also Popkes (1986, 53–91) argues that James is attacking an empty, perverted Paulinism, where faith is a convenient badge for the ambitious (God-fearers) to hide behind, with no intention of fulfilling faith in action. The main thrust of this position is that James (2. 14–26) only really makes sense if it presupposes Paul, but that Paul would himself have agreed with much of James' criticism, even if he would have expressed it somewhat differently. James does not represent an effective attack on Paul's own distinctive, developed theological position. Thus faith as a hollow sham is something that Paul would have failed to recognize as what he preached, and would have deplored as much as James does, while Paul himself frequently insists on faith being lived out in practice. The position that James is attacking stands at least a generation on from Paul, when complacency and nominal faith have taken over from the

---

[10] This needs to be stressed against Adamson 1989, 210–13, who presents a jaundiced view of Judaism.

original fervour of Paul's communities. There is obviously a great deal of affinity between this argument and much of what is represented by (5); so, for example, Bruce argues that, while James does not teach justification by faith as Paul does, he does not contradict Pauline teaching either.[11]

Whether or not James is attacking a later, perverted Paulinism, it is clear that in what he says about faith, and in his theological position as a whole, he is a world apart from Paul. This is the case at least as far as the usual comparison is concerned, that made between 2. 14–26 and Rom. 3–4 (cf. Gal. 3–4). It is worth noting here, however, the interesting argument of Baasland (1982, 127–33), that we need to compare 2. 14–26 not with Rom. 3–4, but with Rom. 2 and 1 Cor. 1–4. This is in many ways a fruitful approach, and consistent with the main thrust of (4) and (5), that James' polemic is something that Paul would agree with; in fact, then Paul and James can be seen to say much the same thing, provided the right material is compared.

Yet, although this overall approach, with all its variations, has much to commend it, there are still problems that obstinately remain. So, for example, Baasland begs the question of James' use of the Abraham paradigm, while many of the other approaches here also fail to do justice to the way James sharply contradicts positions represented by Paul. Hence it is worth considering properly the view of, for example, Hengel (1987) and Lindemann (1979, 240–52), that James is attacking Paul directly. Hengel sees James attacking Paul not just theologically, but also personally (for example, his life style, mission, and means of support). This latter point is unconvincing, but his insistence that there is *real* conflict between Paul and James must be taken seriously. The weakness of this position is the strength of (4) and (5); that James does not systematically or effectively deal with Paul's arguments in Gal. and Rom. But the argument in this case, as Hengel makes

---

[11] Bruce 1952, 76; cf. Heiligenthal 1983, 50, who argues that the focus of Paul's discussion is soteriological, and that of James ecclesiological. As their use of the Abraham tradition shows, they are independent of each other, and cannot simply be compared.

clear, will not be that James is responding to Paul's letters, still less making a considered judgement of them. Instead, it is possible that James is basing his attack on reports that he has received of Paul's preaching.[12] Certainly Paul complains vehemently of being misrepresented (for example, Rom. 3. 8), and it is very probable that false and malicious reports of his preaching and activity were sent, especially to Jerusalem.

In many respects, the difference between these positions is not very great. Whether it is a misrepresented, and hence misunderstood, Paul, a deliberately misunderstood Paul, or a later and perverted Paulinism that is being attacked, it is not Paul's full, distinctive gospel of justification by faith. Yet the idea that James is much more in agreement with Paul than that he is criticizing him, or that the two cannot really be compared, should not be accepted too readily. It runs the risk of blunting James' attack, and of accommodating him too easily to Paul. Central aspects of Paul's gospel really *are* under attack, above all, his claim that God now justifies on the basis of faith alone, and his savage indictment of works. James' response may not engage with Paul's fully developed theology, and may not itself be theologically very profound, but it can still be seen as an attack on a position fundamental to Paul himself. The temptation to make James fit Paul, or not pose any real threat, should be resisted.

However the issue is decided historically, the question still remains of whether, and to what extent, James and Paul are theologically compatible within the canon. The acute tension they create here is not adequately resolved by pushing one of them (usually James!) to the margin.[13] Nor, as I have argued, is it satisfactory to say that James really agrees with Paul, or that he is so different from Paul that the question does not really arise. The argument in this form takes James seriously only to the extent that it seems to clash with Paul. By making Paul the main point of reference, and ensuring that his position

[12] There may also have been reports of letters (especially e.g. Galatians) and of the practice of some Pauline communities (e.g. Corinth).
[13] Lohse 1957, 21–2 allows James a place only on the edge of the canon, and with limited purpose.

remains intact (indeed, if anything, is *supported* by James), it preserves the accepted contours of New Testament theology, with Paul as the yardstick for what is or is not acceptable, and serves to suppress dissident or different voices. It is important both to note the sharp differences and conflict between James and Paul, and also to allow James' own distinctive position to be presented in its own right.

This point has been made by a number of scholars, most notably Eichholz.[14] His main argument is that the theological problem, exposed by Luther and Kirkegaard, is more important than the historical. Hence it is not acceptable to make James stand in Paul's shadow, by evaluating James in terms of Paul, as Luther does. Equally, it is inadequate simply to attempt a harmonization of James and Paul at the outset, especially since such harmonization is impossible and usually works to the detriment of James! In fact James does have a distinctive, if not developed, theology (see ch. 2 and, briefly, ch. 4). Yet even when James' voice has been heard, the problem still remains, as Eichholz rightly says (1953, 48–51), of what Paul and James have to say to each other, since the distinctive theology and emphasis of James' is completely different to that of Paul. Each must be understood in terms of their own task, in their own time, for their own readership. Paul could not have written Jas. 2. 14–26, since the emphasis of his own message, in his own time, for his own audience, is quite different. This is not to relativize Paul, but to say that they cannot simply be reduced to a common denominator.

Childs (1984, 438–43), from his canonical perspective, welcomes Eichholz's approach and looks to develop it further and more positively: Paul and James are to be seen as dealing with different questions from different perspectives. Paul rejects Judaism's claim to derive human salvation from co-operation between divine grace and human good works, since he sees this

---

[14] Eichholz 1953, 5–9, 1961, 37–38. Schlatter 1927, 419 expresses the point succinctly and forcefully: 'It makes no sense to compare James with Paul, before James has been understood.' More ambiguously, Jeremias 1954–5, 371 asserts that James 2 has the right to stand alongside Paul, but immediately modifies this to the right to stand *after* Paul, and says that James' message can only be understood after Paul has been understood!

as a threat to God's freedom. Instead he insists on salvation as wholly an act of divine intervention, with faith as the response. His concern is the relation between the divine and human in acquiring salvation. James, by contrast, is concerned with the relation between the profession of faith and action consonant with it, and, in the face of a split between faith and good works, insists that obedient Christian response to God must combine both faith and righteous behaviour commensurate with God's will. At some times the church will need Paul's primary gospel of salvation by faith alone, and sometimes James' insistence on faith and works as indissolubly linked in faithful response to God. So Childs sees the canonical tension overcome, and the importance of each maintained, in the role of both as witnesses to the one divine revelation of the truth.

There is one further point that Childs (1984, 443-4) makes, again taken up at least partly from Eichholz; that is, the way James serves to show unbroken continuity between Judaism and Christianity, above all in true faith being evident in obedience to the one will of God. The 'Jewishness' of James, and its significance, can usefully be explored further. The other main point of connection for James within the New Testament, apart from Paul, is that of Jesus' teaching in the gospels (see section 1.1.2). James is not passively taking over a set of ethical maxims, but deliberately and creatively using a tradition that lies at the heart of Jesus' proclamation. The main themes of this tradition are that the kingdom belongs to the poor and oppressed (see section 2.1), the rich and powerful are condemned, the kingdom can be anticipated in the way the poor and downcast are treated, God's final judgement is invoked, and the demand is made for true righteousness.[15] James can plausibly be seen both as deliberately taking up the central thrust of Jesus' message and showing its relevance, and also bringing its cutting edge to bear *vis-à-vis* Paul's gospel and the practice of the early communities. In Paul's gospel, the kingdom, concern for the poor, the liberating force of Jesus' message for the immediate material situation, are in danger of

---

[15] Cf. e.g. Maynard-Reid 1987, 81-4; Davids 41-7.

being lost: still more is this the case in the everyday life of the communities. Against this, James stands as a potentially healthy corrective to the (probably inevitable) one-sided emphasis or 'theological abstraction' of Paul.[16]

It may, however, be necessary to go further. The cutting edge of James' message should not be blunted *vis-à-vis* Paul, at several levels. Eichholz, Childs, and others argue very cogently for understanding Paul and James on their own, and not making invidious comparisons, especially as far as James is concerned.[17] But James should not too readily be made anodyne. He may not deal with the full sophisticated Pauline theological position; but he does attack positions that are 'Pauline', and it is difficult to see how he could subscribe to Paul's theology or idea of faith. We may have to choose in the end between James and Paul, rather than simply hold both together.[18] The tension within the canon remains, and cannot simply be wished away.

[16] Jeremias 1954–5, 371 speaks of James fighting against a dead orthodoxy, self-satisfied attitude towards grace, and other symptoms which have constantly devastated congregations of the Pauline type.

[17] E.g. Luck 1984, 3–4 argues that positive Protestant evaluation of James is possible only when, as in the case of Eichholz, Paul and James are made complementary, but that, since all such assessments are concerned only with 2. 14–26, the final evaluation is inevitably negative.

[18] Via 1969, 267 argues that we need in the end to decide between James and Paul. His own preference is for Paul, since James' deficient understanding of faith and human nature leads him to demand works of obedience to the law as a condition of justification, so that unlike Paul he fails to see that this obedience is always turned into a boasting claim upon God. Similarly Baasland 1982, 132 sees Paul as multi-dimensional and James as one-dimensional in their use of faith, works, law, and righteousness, although his assessment of James otherwise, as we have seen, is more positive. Luck 1984, 18 argues that James is imprisoned within a Jewish wisdom tradition that Paul both knows and rejects. If, however, we do need to decide between James and Paul, the choice and criteria may be less simple than Luck and Via seem to think.

CHAPTER 4

James: significance for today

James, as we have seen, has had a troubled history within the Christian tradition, and the verdicts passed on it have been largely negative.[1] The most damning indictment has been that of Luther; his criticisms of James have been massively influential, and that influence is still widespread in contemporary New Testament and wider theological discussion. As we have seen, however, Luther's position here is unsatisfactory. The impression he gives is that James is not being considered as a work in its own right, but is being judged by the criteria of Paul's gospel, above all justification by faith. Because James contradicts Paul on this central issue, its theology must be judged false and misleading, and it should have no place in the New Testament. As we have seen, because James says virtually nothing about Christ or his saving death and resurrection, Luther condemns him for failing to preach the gospel as well as contradicting the true, Pauline gospel.

The problem here is that Luther evaluates James theologically first by the standard of Paul, and secondly for what it does not have, rather than what it does. But, as we saw in the last chapter, even though Luther's treatment of James is seriously question-begging, it is still the case that when we look at James in a more considered and less polemical way, the sense of a deep-rooted confrontation with Paul, and the (or at least a) major thrust of his gospel, will not easily go away. The basic theological problem, at least in this sense, remains acute. And the main attempt to resolve this in modern theological scholar-

---

[1] See further the earlier discussion in e.g. introduction, section 2.2 and ch. 3.

ship, that of Dibelius, raises problems of its own. Dibelius defuses Luther's attack and the harsh judgement on James, as we have seen, by arguing that the two do not come into confrontation theologically at all. This is a very different and fundamentally positive assessment of James. But there still remains, as we have noted, a basic theological problem in this case as well; namely that James really has no theology at all, and again, although for very different reasons, it is effectively pushed to the margins of the canon. If we accept Dibelius' position, that is, then what is theologically important in the New Testament will have to be sought elsewhere, and James will have no part to play.

In some respects the issues involved here loom much less large in contemporary theological discussion. The question of the canon is, for the most part, no longer so central, and the Catholic–Protestant divide that is fundamental to Luther's discussion is not at all so obviously prominent now; both biblically and theologically more generally, it has largely given way to a more ecumenical approach. Nevertheless, James does still look problematic, especially for Lutheran, Protestant theology, and for evangelical Christianity. These traditions variously operate, either implicitly or explicitly, with a 'canon within the canon', and James is excluded from this. For part of the Christian tradition, James can all too easily seem scarcely theologically significant or distinctively Christian.[2]

It is, however, unsatisfactory for James to be shifted from a position of controversy to one of irrelevance. In fact it is a work of potential theological importance within the New Testament, especially for the present day. Certainly it is limited theologically, both in scope and understanding. James does not have a coherent, sustained theological argument (unlike, for example, Hebrews), nor does it represent a major or dominant theological position within the New Testament (in contrast, for example, to Paul or John). It does, however, present firstly an

---

[2] But this generalization does need to be qualified. For a positive and often impressive interpretation of James from an evangelical perspective see especially Adamson 1989; also Davids 1982; Martin 1988; and, from a Lutheran position, Eichholz 1953, 1961 is especially notable.

urgent address and warning, and secondly a *demand for the true and full practice of the faith*, for the living out of the implications of the message, and for the demonstrating of the distinctive nature of the community.[3]

This above all is why James should be taken seriously now. It is this urgent summons to live out the faith that is acutely relevant for the present day. James does not have everything that is necessary for the present-day formulation of Christian theology or working out of the Christian faith. Nor is it clear how much of the gospel, or what gospel precisely, James presupposes.[4] But, in its emphasis on helping those in need, the poor, the oppressed, the unimportant, it is crucially relevant for present-day Christianity.

It is also the case that James does have its own theological profile, even if it is difficult in some respects to recognise or articulate this, and even if it is not worked out as a full, still less sophisticated, theology. It may be that James is to be seen as providing conventional paraenetical advice and not rounded theological formulations for his audience, and as a primitive Christian teacher, not a theologian of the first rank, compared with Paul. But, as Eichholz rightly says, since when should the voice of the layman not be heard in the church?![5] We need to take the positive and negative main theological positions of James very seriously.

First, and most distinctively in the New Testament, James lays considerable positive emphasis on *works* (but *not* 'works of the law', in the pejorative Pauline sense, or limited to Jewish cultic observance, food-laws, or circumcision). This emphasis is there from the start and represents the basic thrust of the whole letter; works is the key word for James, just as faith is for Paul.[6]

---

[3] See further e.g. Popkes 1986, 126–56, 207–10.

[4] M. J. Townsend, 'Christ, Community and Salvation in the Epistle of James', *EvQ* 53 (1981) 115–23, follows C. F. D. Moule, *Worship in the New Testament*, London, 1961, 65, in seeing James as presupposing the preaching of the (central themes of the) gospel.

[5] Eichholz 1953; 35; see further 31–5 on the question of James' theological 'profile' or 'contours'.

[6] Cf. Eichholz 1961, 38, even though (as he notes and as we have already seen) James does not have a fully developed theology of works; cf. Blondel 1979, 147.

The constant theme of this is the importance of living out faith in action, and not merely professing it, and the focus is above all on acts of mercy, constant concern for others, living faithfully to the nature of God and (implicitly) the distinctive message of Christ. All this is portrayed as central and indispensable to the Christian community, both individually and collectively; it is the *sine qua non* of authentic Christian existence and true discipleship.

Secondly, and correspondingly, James provides a positive portrayal of faith, in the sense of deep, absolute trust in, and commitment to, God, as shown by the whole way of life (above all in works and acts of mercy), and which is not, negatively, a mere bland assertion of belief or credal correctness. Popkes claims that for James faith denotes the whole of human life lived in obedience to the divine word; but Blondel is right to see this as true of Paul but not of James. Although James does have a more positive concept of faith than is often realised, faith must still be defined and perfected by works, and works is the important theme throughout. Again Blondel rightly argues that the problem of faith and works for James is not the alternative they pose, but the absurdity of their separation.[7]

So, thirdly, James lays stress on the keeping and living out of faith in difficult and testing circumstances; this is urged both in face of a hostile, alien world and ultimate testing, and also in relation to mundane, everyday difficulties and temptations.[8]

Fourthly, James represents more than anything else in the New Testament the challenge of the continuity of the Jewish inheritance, and an argument potentially for the importance of the common ground between Judaism and Christianity and the lack of any essential divide between them. James can, in this sense, be seen as making a case for Christianity, as Judaism, to be primarily concerned not with belief, but

---

[7] See Eichholz 1953, 49; Blondel 1979, 148. As the latter points out, justification by faith alone for James is negative, in contrast to Paul.

[8] Perdue 1981 argues that this theme belongs integrally to the process of socialization and legitimation of the world into which members of the community have entered.

practice, the people of God living in complete obedience to the divine command. James, amongst other things, offers considerable scope for common ground and dialogue with Judaism.

Fifthly, James carries forward some of the central aspects of Jesus' message and teaching, not just ethically (as with the close connections with the Sermon on the Mount traditions), but also in preserving something of the vision of the kingdom and the new age, and (bound up with this) of the gospel being for the poor and oppressed, and of God being on the side of the poor and vulnerable.[9] This continuity with Jesus' teaching is relatively rare within the New Testament, and James stands as an important witness to one possible line of development for the Christian community, against the direction taken by the majority of early writers and communities. Here there are strong links with, and support for, the central theme of liberation theology, in its 'preferential option for the poor'. Thus far liberation theology has made little use of James, but potentially James has a great deal to offer.

Above all, then, the theological significance of James for today is to be found in the constant, sustained attack on the rich and powerful, and the upholding of the cause of the poor and oppressed. It provides a fundamental criticism of injustice and violence and demands respect for the poor, not the state or secular authorities.[10] This may not be theologically sophisticated, but it is not naïve either. It stands in essential continuity with the Old Testament prophetic tradition and the central thrust of Jesus' message of the kingdom. It lays bare the power interests involved in human relationships, actions, and words, and calls the bluff of falsely motivated action. Against this, it calls for genuine faith and concrete, practical action. Both for its own time, and also for the present day, it poses a challenge to society and to the Christian community.

The theological thrust of James goes deeper than may at first

---

[9] H. J. Held, 'Glaube ohne "Ansehen der Person". Zu Jakobus 2, 1–13', in: G. Metzger (ed.), *Zukunft aus dem Wort*, Stuttgart 1978, 209–25, presents a sustained argument for James as portraying God on the side of the poor, against discrimination. See also Maynard-Reid 1987.

[10] Cf. Popkes 1986, 197–9.

appear. Certainly, as I said in the Introduction, the theological significance of James should not be exaggerated, and Popkes (1986, 209–10) rightly notes that James cannot form the basis of Christian theology. But, as he immediately goes on to say, James does contain much that is basic to Christian theology, and it would have been better for Luther to make positive use of James than to dismiss it as he did. James' theology may be deficient and inadequate in some respects, but it offers insights that must not be overlooked. For example, it can serve as an important corrective to many aspects of the contemporary emphasis in Western Christianity on spirituality. In contrast to the individualizing and detached attitude to the world that this can easily lead to, James points the way to the essence of authentic Christian existence, in the living out of faith, self-giving love, and communal concern for others, especially the poor, outcasts, and despised. So, more generally, James ruthlessly exposes the glaring contradictions of the church and individual Christians, especially the lack of correlation between belief and practice, and a church threatened by the fact that its everyday life contradicts its profession of Christian faith.

Probably the Christian church has always needed to hear this message and address these problems. But this need is above all acute in our modern, secular, pluralistic age. Christianity can provide no convincing concrete answers in face of the massive global and individual problems that threaten humanity. It has nothing distinctive to offer; that is probably a considerable part of the appeal of spirituality, since it provides an attractive and distinctive perspective in contrast to popular obsession with acquisitive materialism. However this may be, the fact is that Christianity has no reason to be taken seriously if it fails to live out its faith at real cost to itself (financially, socially, and emotionally), and therefore represent a real challenge to the complacency and deep helplessness of modern Western society. Even here, it may not necessarily represent a distinctive attitude or voice in the present world; others may live in much the same sort of way from very different perspectives. But it is still indispensable for the individual and the church to live out their faith in this way, even if it is not all that this faith involves or that the church needs to articulate and reflect upon. In the end, the real danger in interpreting James for the present-day is not that we might promote a crude or naïve theology over against the profundity of Paul, but that we explain away or diminish the full force of James too easily. Christianity and Christian theology ignore the message of James at their peril.[11]

---

[11] Cf. Schlatter 1932, 7; Popkes 1986, 209–10.

References

Adamson, J. B., 1976: *The Epistle of James*, Grand Rapids.
    1989: *James: the Man and his Message*, Grand Rapids.
Baasland, E., 1982: 'Der Jakobusbrief als neutestamentliche Weisheitsschrift', *ST* 36, 119–39.
Bieder, W., 1949: 'Christliche Existenz nach dem Zeugnis des Jakobusbriefes', *TZ* 5, 93–113.
Blondel, J.-L., 1979: 'Le fondement théologique de la parénèse dans l'épître de Jacques', *RTP* 29, 141–52.
Bruce, F. F., 1952: 'Justification by Faith in the Non-Pauline Writings of the New Testament', *EvQ* 2, 66–77.
Burchard, C., 1980a: 'Zu Jakobus 2, 14–26', *ZNW* 71, 27–45.
    1980b: 'Gemeinde in der strohernen Epistel. Mutmassungen über Jakobus', in: D. Lührmann and G. Strecker (eds.), *Kirche*, Tübingen.
Childs, B. S., 1984: *The New Testament as Canon: an Introduction*, London.
Davids, P. H., 1982: *The Epistle of James*, Grand Rapids.
Davies, W. D., 1964: *The Setting of the Sermon on the Mount*, Cambridge.
Dibelius-Greeven, 1976: M. Dibelius (rev. H. Greeven), *A Commentary on the Epistle of James*, Philadelphia.
Eichholz, G., 1953: *Jakobus und Paulus*, Munich.
    1961: *Glaube und Werk bei Jakobus und Paulus*, Munich.
Hartin, P., 1991: *James and the Q Sayings of Jesus* (JSNTSS 47), Sheffield.
Heiligenthal, R., 1983: *Werke als Zeichen* (WUNT 2. 9), Tübingen.
Hengel, M., 1987: 'Der Jakobusbrief als antipaulinische Polemik', in: G. F. Hawthorn and O. Betz (eds.), *Tradition and Interpretation in the New Testament*, Tübingen/Grand Rapids.

Hoppe, R., 1977: *Der theologische Hintergrund des Jakobusbriefes*, Würzburg.

Jeremias, J., 1954–5: 'Paul and James', *ExpTim* 66, 368–71.

Johnson, L. T., 1982: 'The Use of Leviticus in the Letter of James', *JBL* 101, 391–401.

Laws, S., 1980: *A Commentary on the Epistle of James*, London.

Lindemann, A., 1979: *Paulus im ältesten Christentum* (BHT 58), Tübingen.

Lohse, E., 1957: 'Glaube und Werke – zur Theologie des Jakobus', *ZNW* 48, 1–22.

Luck, U., 1984: 'Die Theologie des Jakobusbriefes', *ZTK* 81, 1–30.

Marcus, J., 1982: 'The Evil Inclination in the Epistle of James', *CBQ* 44, 606–21.

Martin, R. P., 1988: *James*, Waco.

Maynard-Reid, P. U., 1987: *Poverty and Wealth in James*, Maryknoll.

Mayor, J. B., 1913: *The Epistle of St. James*, London.

Mussner, F., 1970: '"Direkte" und "indirekte" Christologie im Jakobusbrief', *Cath* 24, 111–16.

1981: *Der Jakobusbrief*, Freiburg.

Obermüller, R., 1972: 'Hermeneutische Themen im Jakobusbrief', *Bib* 53, 234–44.

Perdue, L. G., 1981: 'Paraenesis and the Epistle of James', *ZNW* 72, 241–56.

Popkes, W., 1986: *Adressaten, Situation und Form des Jakobusbriefes*, Stuttgart.

Ropes, J. H., 1916: *A Critical and Exegetical Commentary on the Epistle of St. James*, Edinburgh.

Schlatter, A., 1927: *Der Glaube im Neuen Testament*, Stuttgart.

1932: *Der Brief des Jakobus*, Stuttgart.

Via, D. O., 1969: 'The Right Strawy Epistle Reconsidered', *JR* 49, 253–67.

Weiss, K., 1976: 'Motiv und Ziel der Frömmigkeit des Jakobusbriefes', *ThV* 7, 107–14.

II

The Theology of Jude, 1 Peter, and 2 Peter

RALPH P. MARTIN

CHAPTER 5

Jude

THE SETTING OF THE LETTER

Containing one chapter of 25 verses, the letter of Jude is one of the shortest in the New Testament, with a vocabulary of only 227 words. The author claims to be 'Jude ... the brother of James' (1), a claim – if taken at face value – that puts him in the Holy Family of the Lord as being also a brother of Jesus. He is then the person mentioned in Matthew 13. 55 and Mark 6. 3 in the company of the 'brothers' of Jesus. Other people named Juda(s) are present in the New Testament story, but the other clear rival,[1] Judas as one of the Twelve (Luke 6. 16; Acts 1. 13) or Thaddeus (Matt. 10. 3//Mark 3. 18 with the variant Lebbaeus) is not really a candidate for authorship if we take the description 'brother of James' seriously. Only one person on the stage of apostolic history qualifies to be regarded as both James' brother and a servant of the Lord Jesus, assuming 'James' is that member of the Holy Family (Gal. 1. 19). In Christian history (preserved by Hegesippus, according to Eusebius, *Church History* 3. 19. 1–20. 1–8) a tradition that places Jude within early Palestinian Christianity is attested, along with the role ascribed to James.

Not all scholars follow these conclusions, although some recent investigation has made the identification plausible.[2] If,

---

[1] For one other possibility which identifies the Jude of the letter with Judas in Acts 15. 22, 27 see E. E. Ellis, *Prophecy and Hermeneutic in Early Christianity*, Grand Rapids, 1978, 226–8; or a Jude as third bishop of Jerusalem, according to *Apostolic Constitutions* 7. 46.

[2] See R. J. Bauckham, in his most recent contribution *Jude and the Relatives of Jesus in the Early Church*, Edinburgh 1990; see too his *Commentary on Jude, 2 Peter*, WBC 50, Waco 1983.

on other grounds such as style and the nature of the false teaching opposed, the letter is dated later than the era of the Holy Family's life within Palestinian Christianity, then the name Jude is a literary device to give authority to a pseudonymous work.[3] On this view, the author is unknown, or else a disciple of Jude, the Lord's brother, as Pierre Reymond thinks.[4]

The setting of the letter, on balance, is more likely to be early Palestinian Christianity than in the period of the second century which is where those who regard the letter as a pseudograph tend to place it. Yet the main issue is not one of authorship and dating; rather it is to be found with the purpose of the letter and the nature of the false teaching it was designed to repel.

The letter of Jude is basically a polemical document.[5] Framed by a richly worded salutation to 'those who are called, beloved in God the Father and kept safe for Jesus Christ' (1), and the concluding doxology (24–5) which is one of the most fulsome in the whole New Testament, the body of the letter is carefully constructed. The occasion and theme are stated (3–4), giving both an encouragement which motivates the author (3) and a warning (4) that centres on the false teachers.

The letter proper opens at 5, where the first of four prophecies of doom borrowed largely from the Old Testament heralds the character and fate of Jude's enemies in the church. This section extends to 19. Thereafter the four sentences of doom earlier set down are matched by four exhortations to Christian behaviour (20–1) leading to a final admonition on the way the waverers and lapsed are to be dealt with (22–3). The closing doxology (24–5) is built on the author's confidence that his readers will remain faithful and true, kept by divine power (a thought reverting to 1).

---

[3] The pseudepigraphic character of Jude is taken as undisputed in R. Heiligenthal's survey, 'Der Judasbrief', *ThR* 51/2 (1986), 117–29 (120). But see an objection to this as too optimistic in Bauckham, *Jude and the Relatives*, 174, n. 262.

[4] P. Reymond, *L'épître de saint Jude*, CNT, Neuchâtel 1980, 148.

[5] J. N. D. Kelly, *A Commentary*, 228 speaks of 'straightforward polemical tract'; K. H. Schelke, *Der Judasbrief*, Herders Theologischer Kommentar, 13 Freiburg, 1961, 137 calls it an 'antihäretisches Flugblatt.'

The central section 4 to 19 carries the weight of the writer's message. It follows a well-known pattern of 'text and interpretation', in which an authoritative message is followed by an interpretative application to the readers' own day. The theme, however, is consistently the same throughout these four 'words of doom'. The false teachers who have recently appeared on the scene are the latest examples of other ungodly characters whose fate and judgement has long since been executed. Prophecies look back to earlier fulfilment, as a warning to present-day readers.

Even so, the argument and arrangements of the material are closely woven in artistic shape. This feature suggests that the popular notion that Jude 'apparently felt no need to refute' the teaching of his opponents. 'He only vituperates against them'[6] is far from the mark. He has opponents in his sights throughout, and engages them in debate, if indirectly. We turn now to see how this argumentation proceeds.

THE PLAN OF THE LETTER

1. Opening salutation (1–2)
Jude identifies himself and greets his readers with a confident tone and an expression of divine mercy, peace and love.

2. Occasion and aim of the Letter (3–4)
The author has felt impelled to divert his attention from his original purpose which was to write about a shared salvation; instead he addresses an admonition to engage in a fight on behalf of the apostolic faith, now threatened and soon to be recalled (17). The occasion for the writing is then explicitly spelled out: it is the infiltration of false teachers who are branded for their immoral ways and assault on the church's Lord. The aim is to warn of this attack and to expose it for what Jude claims to be: a denial of apostolic teaching by those who follow 'their own desires' (16, 18).

---

[6] J. L. Price, *The New Testament. Its History and Theology*, New York 1987, 412; cf. Kelly, *Commentary*, 223.

3. The body of the letter (5–23)

This is the central section and falls into two distinct parts. *Part one* extends from 5 to 19 and is a carefully fashioned statement of an authoritative text followed by an application to the readers' situation. *Part two* (20–3) is exhortation directed to the readers, calling on them to stand firm and take action, if we may borrow the language of Daniel 11. 32 (NRSV) in a similar context of encouragement when trials threaten and the temptation to succumb to wrongheaded ideas is apparent.

4. Closing doxology (24–5)

This magnificent benediction is formed by a bringing together of a tribute raised to God's favour on believers' behalf and an ascription of what God's character is in itself. So 24 describes God's actions, while 25 enumerates the qualities that belong to God, as Reymond remarks.[7]

Divine power is at work to hold Jude's loyal readers in safety against seductive appeals, and to bring them to their eschatological salvation in joy (21). The power to do this resides in, and is drawn from, the unique and saving God made known in the unique Master and Lord (4), Jesus Christ. All praise, expressed in fulsome, liturgical idioms, is addressed to this God.

FALSE TEACHERS IN JUDE[8]

The previous section has already touched on the types of belief and practice Jude seeks to expose and repel. Now it is helpful to gather together the scattered allusions into a coherent whole to see if we can fix an identity label on the teachers who had encroached on the assembly. If we can understand the claims they were making and the danger they posed in Jude's eyes, this will give us a point of entry into Jude's theological and moral perspectives. It is clear that what he writes is in reaction to the threat he perceived; and the teaching he finds objection-

---

[7] Reymond, *L'épître*, 188.
[8] For this topic the most recent discussion, with bibliography, is G. Sellin, 'Die Häretiker des Judasbriefes,' *ZNW* 76–7 (1985–6) 207–25, to which I am indebted.

able acts as a foil to set forth his own contributions of a doctrinal and pastoral character.

The indictments Jude brings against these persons are expressed in a kaleidoscope of colourful terms, among which the following are the most vivid:

(1) 'These dreamers' (8). The term suggests that their teaching is no better than what is invented out of their visions or trance-like ecstasies. The main point is found in their slander of the angels which is treated in 9–10, which in turn looks back to 6–7. The common thread running through these enigmatic allusions to the angels seems to be the way the false teaching refused to keep human existence (called 'the flesh', *sarx* in 8) and angelic existence apart. In ancient thought angels and humans were imagined as belonging to two separate worlds with quite distinct 'spheres' of both habitation and influence. The error Jude is concerned to repel was evidently a bid to run these two worlds together and to fantasize that human beings were like angels, with the intended consequence that they used this device as a justification for their advocating immoral ways (4). There is a point of contact with 1 Corinthians in which Paul's controversy with Corinthian enthusiasts conceivably turned on the nature of Christian existence and their attitude to 'the flesh', i.e. human nature. For the Corinthians, who imagined that they had already become like the angels and so were free from all earthly constraints following their baptismal resurrection (1 Cor. 4. 8), the claims of morality were treated with an attitude that Paul cannot condone, especially when it led to pride (1 Cor. 5. 2, 6) and sexual/bodily indulgence (1 Cor. 6. 12–20). Paul issued a warning that there is still a 'not-yet' tension between salvation already secured in Christ and its future perfection at the parousia of Christ (1 Cor. 15. 20–8). The practice of 'tongues of angels' (1 Cor. 13. 1) used to praise God ecstatically (as in *Apoc. Abraham* 15. 6; *Test. Job* 48–50) needs this reminder of an eschatological proviso; and, even in the final attainment of salvation, the line between humans and angels will not be forgotten (1 Cor. 6. 3: 'we are to judge angels'). We may compare the rivalry-motive between mortals and angels in rabbinic Judaism (Slav Enoch 22).

(2) 'Blemishes on your love-feasts' (12) repeats the thought of the teachers' presence and influence as 'defiling' (8) and looks ahead to 23, 'hating even the tunic defiled by the flesh'. This curious phrase speaks of the staining of an inner garment as it is brought into contact with dirt. The human body is affected as well. Jude uses the vivid imagery of the way moral evil has power to contaminate once its influence is left unchecked. The line of thought is parallel with 1 Cor. 5 where Paul calls for a drastic handling of a moral situation and 'separation' from evil.

Assuming the teachers came from outside Jude's congregation, as 4 (NRSV) implies, they were evidently able to gain access to the congregation's inner life and share the agape meals, convivial gatherings where the believers met to share food and drink as a prelude to the solemn remembrance of the Lord's death. The practice of a common meal is supported by the evidence in Acts 2. 46; 1 Cor. 11. 17–34; and in the churches of the Didache (chs. 9–10) and Ignatius (*Smyrn*. 8. 2; cf. *Acts of Paul and Thecla* 25) as well as the setting of 2 Peter 2:13. The intruding teachers (see 4) acted out of irreverence and in a selfish manner, regarding only their own interests akin to the ways of the false shepherds of Ezek. 34. Their mercenary motives and self-interest show their affinity with the spirit that moved Balaam (11) with his cupidity and deceit.

A cluster of evocative images in 12–13 really amounts to two exposures. Stated in prosaic terms, they are unable to make good on the promises they offer, just like clouds that suggest a rainfall that never comes (a sad disappointment in the climatic conditions of the Middle East, when rain is needed to ensure a harvest) or trees that are barren at the fruit-bearing season. Second, they lack stability and are as unsteady as the restless sea (an imagery drawn from Isa. 57. 20 and applied to false teachers in Eph. 4. 14) and as untrustworthy as stars that fail to hold their course and so mislead the navigator (a point in 'wayward stars' that reverts to 6 where the angels, often thought of as stars in 1 Enoch, moved out of their God-appointed domain and so fell, like Lucifer, Isa. 14. 12–20. Jude can promise no worse fate for these opponents than a blackest doom of judgement.

(3) 'These men' – a reiterated literary device, repeated five times in the verses we are using to gain a profile – 'are grumblers and complainers' (16). The object of their sour-spirited attack is evidently God, once the Old Testament parallels to these words are observed (Exod. 16. 7–12; Num. 14. 27, 29; 17. 5, 10). That point is clinched by the preceding citation of 1 Enoch 1. 9 with its exposure of the 'ungodly' (a term repeated in four different ways) as those guilty of 'harsh things which ungodly sinners have spoken against him' (God). The text of 1 Enoch is reworked in Jude's statement but it is retained exactly as in 1 Enoch 1. 9 in the closing sentence; and the stress on 'ungodly' is made by the use of the word three times. Obviously 'ungodliness' (*asebeia*⁹) is a watchword shared by Jude and 1 Enoch, and is linked in 1 Enoch with the trait of 'denial' as in 'denying the name of the Lord of the Spirits' (1 Enoch 38. 2; 41. 2; 45. 2; 46. 7; 48. 10). The same connection may be seen in Jude 4, 'disowning our only Master and Lord Jesus Christ', which links with 1 Enoch 48. 10: the ungodly have 'denied the Lord of the Spirits and his Anointed One'.¹⁰

Their pride is shown by the arrogant speech that Jude calls boasting (16) and elsewhere slander against heavenly beings (8, 10). Their attitude demonstrates the way they are at the mercy of their instincts and (evil) desires. This has led them into immoral ways, which they practise evidently on the ground that they are driven to their licence by their 'fate' (the unusual adjective rendered 'complainers' carries the idea of blaming other people for one's lot and so excusing oneself for actions beyond one's control).

⁹ This catchword is difficult to define. Sellin, 'Die Häretiker', 211 makes out a good case for taking it as general licentiousness and excess, though 8 has been interpreted as an allusion to erotic dreams, as with Clem. Alex. *somniant imaginatione sua libidines* (cited in Reymond, 166 n. 12). *Sarx*, flesh, probably has a wider meaning and refers to religious visions set up in opposition to angelic authority, Sellin, 'Die Häretiker', 213–14.

¹⁰ For the use made of Enoch see now J. Daryl Charles, 'Jude's Use of Pseudepigraphical Source-Material as Part of a Literary Strategy', *NTS* 37 (1991) 130–45. See too M. Black, 'The Maranatha Invocation and Jude 14, 15 (1 Enoch 1:9)', in *Christ and Spirit in the New Testament*. Studies in Honour of C. F. D. Moule. (eds.) B. Lindars and S. S. Smalley, Cambridge 1973, 189–96; C. D. Osburn, 'The Christological Use of 1 Enoch 1:9 in Jude 14, 15', *NTS* 23 (1976–7) 334–41.

(4) The designation 'scoffers' (18) picks up initially the way of life the teachers adopt, since the opprobrium of the term is connected to the following of their own desires for ungodly things. But a specific meaning attaches to the label Jude fastens on them in view of the apocalyptic introduction to 18: 'In the last time there will be . . . ' Evidently the teaching opposed here has to do with the denial of apocalyptic elements in the Christian message either by way of a spiritualizing device that in turn arose of the teachers' belief that the fulness of salvation was achieved here and now, or a general scepticism, mirrored in, but not identical with 2 Peter 3. 3, that cast doubt on the hope of a future parousia of the Lord. The same Greek word for 'mockers, scoffers' in both Jude and 2 Peter indicates that the point of issue was eschatological, a fact of some theological importance. In Jude the teachers denied the reality of judgement, in 2 Peter they questioned on other grounds (3. 4) the delay of the final advent: 'What has become of the promise of his coming?' The same appeal is made in both documents to the teaching of the apostles as a fountainhead of authority. We find here an allegation that the teachers were deemed to have set themselves up as rival authorities who sought to undermine Jude's adherence to what he believed to be pure doctrine, handed down from a venerable source (3). Jude does not align himself directly with the apostles; rather he makes an appeal to them as authority figures who ought to be recognized by the congregation. Jude's relationship to his readers is warm and personal. The repetition of 'beloved' in the paragraph of 17–23 is notable, reverting to 3 with its call also to the 'beloved' ones of his audience.

(5) The final indication of the nature of the opposition Jude confronts comes in 19, which in many ways both sums up and judges the type of teaching in his sights: 'These [men] are those who cause divisions, they are worldly minded (rendering *psychikoi*[11]), they do not have the Spirit.' The schismatic tendency is obvious, since their influence was evidently a source of

---

[11] B. A. Pearson, *The Pneumatikos-Psychikos Terminology in 1 Corinthians*, SBLDS 12, Chico, CA, 1973; R. A. Horsley, 'Pneumatikos vs. Psychikos. Distinctions of Spiritual Status Among the Corinthians', *HTR* 69 (1976) 269–88.

consternation within the Jude congregation, and set the faithful in opposition to their fellow-believers. Jealousy and strife are the inevitable concomitants of a teaching that maintained a distinction between an elite group and ordinary Christians, as at Corinth (1 Cor. 3. 3) and in James' congregations (Jas. 3. 14). Interestingly both these indictments trace back the root-cause to the presence of *psychikoi*, people gripped by worldly influences which stand in direct contrast to the power of the (Holy) Spirit in human lives (1 Cor. 2. 14; 15: 46; Jas. 3. 15; 4. 5). Both contrasts draw on a theology of wisdom[12] which is the Spirit's gift and enables mortals to know God and live in peace and harmony. Jude's thrust against his opponents shares the same background, as he moves to brand the opposition not only as unspiritual (in spite of its claim to be gifted with superior knowledge of heavenly realities, 10), but also as definitely lacking the Spirit altogether. Their pretensions to esoteric wisdom and unbridled freedom – seen in their disdain of the angels and their immoral practices – are condemned, in Jude's invective, as unChristian, and so lacking in any claim to acceptance. The teachers are no better than 'irrational creatures', living on a purely natural plane (10) and with a bid to 'know' that lacks understanding and borders on blasphemy.

In attempting to sum up the nature of the opposition Jude encountered we note that, as with most rival teaching denounced by apostolic writers generally, there are two sides: a theoretical and a practical. The sectarian teaching in this epistle, as judged by the writer, is no exception. The doctrinal basis touched on such issues as a belief that Christian salvation was already fully experienced, with a consequent denial of the apocalyptic elements that looked to a yet-uncompleted future. This realized eschatology was matched with a mystical approach to God in terms of ecstasy and spiritual awareness that, in its immediacy, poured scorn on the angels, evidently regarded in Jude's church as mediators.[13] The 'spiritualizing'

---

[12] R. P. Martin, *James*, WBC, Waco 1988, 128–38, and lxxxii–lxxxiv; cf. Sellin, 'Die Häretiker', 218, 220.

[13] Sellin, 'Die Häretiker', 221–2 wants to see a direct link with Col. 2. 18–19, taken to reflect an anti-angel bias by some members of an enthusiastic wing of Paul's school.

of religion – as no doubt the teachers deemed it – was thought to be the counterpart of God's pure grace (4) that replaced any moral requirements for 'staying in' salvation, a notion akin to that expressed in Romans 3. 8; 6. 1–14, as well as the parallel section in 2 Peter 2. 19 with its promise of unrestricted freedom. At stake, according to Jude, is an attack on divine authority as centred in the apostolic tradition (17) and the deposit of the faith (3, 20), and a denial of the moral issues that God's judgement on sinners illustrates (5–7). Yet the main critique Jude makes of the teachers is that they denied the only Master and Lord, Jesus Christ (4), and showed an attitude of rebellious unbelief (5). On both counts they merit judgement which will be swift in its execution.

The use of the legend, drawn from a variety of Jewish sources, in 9 (see Bauckham's full note in his *Commentary*) to the effect that Michael did not dare to condemn the devil in dispute over Moses' body, has the same point in mind. It is that the teachers, in disowning the true sovereign Lord Jesus, end up with only their own self-regarding autonomy. Michael's case ought to have warned them that not even the archangel presumes to arrogate the role of judge to himself; he too must submit the case to the Lord, who is the sole arbiter.

The practical implications of the alien teaching are even clearer. Basically the cavalier attitude to morality, on the mistaken ground that being ranked with the enlightened *psychikoi*, or falsely claimed 'spiritual' people (19) was a passport to ethical indifference (4), led to Jude's severe warning. God's grace may be perverted into licence, and the teachers evidently confused 'freedom from sin' with 'freedom to sin', a false step indicated in 2 Peter 2. 19. The teachers' ways are condemned as godless (4, 14–16) and ripe for future judgement (4, 7, 13) which has already begun (10). Nor can Jude forbear to bring standard accusations against them for their selfwilled notions (akin to Cain's impiety and rebel spirit as judged by Jewish

This would range Jude's opponents with a group standing in the Pauline tradition – a most unlikely connection, given the strict moralism of Col. 3. Links with the extreme Pauline enthusiasts debated in Jam. 2. 14–24 are a more promising line of inquiry (Sellin, 'Die Häretiker', 211 n. 17 and R. P. Martin, *James* 75–101).

writings such as Philo, Josephus, and Targums[14] as well as Gen. 4), their avarice and deceit (illustrated by Balaam's example and error, according to Num. 22–4) and their pride (exemplified in Korah's opposition to Moses, in Num. 16).

These teachers were presumably itinerant prophets akin to those in Didache chs. 11–13. Points of similarity are in their arrival and acceptance among the Jewish Christian believers (4), in the hospitality they evidently received and abused (12), if the reference to the 'profit' they gained (11) is taken at face value, and in their charismatic authority which they exploited by setting themselves against apostolic traditions that Jude embodied. The 'tunic defiled by the flesh' (23), which has a figurative meaning, may conceivably also be a pointed allusion to their garment, the clothing of the itinerant charismatic prophet following in the steps of the original disciples of Jesus (Mark 6. 9; Matt. 10. 10), as well as the Cynic wandering philosopher (Diogenes Laert. 6. 13).[15]

JUDE'S THEOLOGICAL RESPONSES

The writer's reaction to the menace is such that he felt moved to turn away from his originally intended project and address a warning with the rival, intruding teachers clearly in view (3). The counter arguments he brings out are designed to engage the teachers in polemics; but more clearly they are directed to the congregation as a pastoral and persuasive call to stand firm in the apostolic faith (3), to take steps to ensure their continuance in that faith (20–1), and to be concerned about their fellow-believers who have been seduced (22–3). Jude's pastoral theology is shaped by three chief considerations.

1. He underscores the need to maintain adherence to the teaching already given by, and derived from, the apostles themselves (3, 17, 20). The 'faith once delivered to the saints' is

[14] Philo, *On the Posterity of Cain* 38–9, 42; *Migration of Abraham* 75; Josephus, *Antiquities* 1. 52ff; Targum of Jonathan on Gen. 4. 7.
[15] See Sellin, 'Die Häretiker', 233–4 who makes a lot of the use of *chiton*, an inner garment, as a badge of wandering prophets (see BAGD s.v.). On the general question of itinerant charismatic figures in Palestinian Christianity, see G. Theissen, *The First Followers of Jesus*, London 1978.

a strong assertion of *fides quae creditur*, that is, faith seen as a body of belief, however rudimentary, that enshrined the tenets of Christian salvation and that must be defended and not surrendered, especially when other teachings are being canvassed. Jude does not use Paul's language, which prefers terms like the 'gospel' (Phil. 1. 7, 27; Rom. 2. 16; 16. 25 (if authentic); 1 Cor. 15. 1–2); 'the faith' (Phil. 1. 27; Col. 2. 6–7; cf. Eph. 4. 5; 1 Tim. 6. 20–1); 'the truth' (Col. 1. 5; cf. 2 Thess. 2. 13; 2 Tim. 2. 18, 25; 4. 4); 'the apostolic traditions' (1 Cor. 11.2; 15. 1–2; Gal. 1. 9; Col. 2. 6; 1 Thess. 4. 1; cf. 2 Thess. 2. 15). Other allusions to a corpus of distinctive doctrine, held to be a sacred deposit from God, are 'the apostles' teaching' (Acts 2. 42); 'the standard of teaching' (Rom. 6. 17); 'the words of faith and good doctrine' (1 Tim. 4. 6); 'the pattern of sound words' (2 Tim. 1. 13); and 'sound teaching' (2 Tim. 4. 3; Tit. 1. 9).

These diverse references give the impression of a web of saving truth and moral guidelines which provided for early believers the 'way' by which their new life in Christ was to be understood and practised. (Note the contrast in 11: the way of Cain.)

Granted that these traditions were still loosely assembled and covered a wide variety of responses to Christian believing and living, it still remains the case that such formulations were intended to be respected and held firm, especially in time of doubt and assault when the tendency to deny them and to follow rival patterns was marked. Jude 3 gives us one of the clearest illustrations of a development within early Christianity when 'the faith' is being crystallized and set in fairly rigid forms, buttressed by the appeal to antiquity and to be battled for with vehemence and vigour. The consolidation of doctrine is not expressed yet in terms that resemble the ethos and strategy in, say, 1 Clement, Ignatius, and the later Apologists of the mid-second century.

Scholars use the label 'early Catholicism' to denote this emergent tendency to find in institutional forms and procedures an essential basis for the church's life. If that is the definition of 'early Catholicism' it is obvious that the tone and temper of Jude's appeal do not betray an indebtedness to this type of ecclesiastical argument or non-apocalyptic under-standing of the Christian faith. On the contrary Jude's thrust is to extol the apocalyptic elements in defence of a forward-looking hope (21) and a Spirit-controlled expression of the faith (20).

The one point, however, at which Jude does show a marked development, is his giving to 'faith' (in addition to the more existential dimension found in the negative aspect of 5) a shape that portrays it as preservation of the once-for-all deposit (as in Polycarp, *Phil.* 3. 2). But *pistis* (faith) still retains its eschatolo-gical character, while incorporating the extra dimension of being a virtue of steadfastness and loyalty (akin to 2 Pet. 1. 15–17) – a trait also found in the Pauline and other NT letters (for example, 1 Cor. 16. 13; Gal. 3. 23, 25; 6. 10; Phil. 1. 25; Col. 1. 23; Heb. 3. 6, 14; 4. 14; 10. 23). Yet there is little in his short letter to link Jude with the setting of the church as highly organized and structured. The 'predictions of the apostles' (17) refer to traditions derived from the Lord's representatives, not the apostles holding a formal office or teaching position. The situation is more akin to that in 1 Cor. than in the Aposto-lic fathers like Ignatius and 1 Clement.

2. The role of Jesus as judge underlines the two emphases Jude strove to make clear: God acts through Jesus, and God's character includes that of judgement. The test-case comes in 5 with its reminder of how 'the Lord saved a people from the land of Egypt[16] and afterwards destroyed those who disbe-lieved'. The warning note of doom is clearly sounded, called forth by the disbelief of the teachers in 4. What is interesting is the way some textual authorities read 'God', 'Jesus' (or 'Joshua') for 'the Lord'. The latter indicates that the human agent of divine doom was either Jesus in his pre-existence or as typified in the successor to Moses who carried his name.

---

[16] The textual issues presented in 5 are considerable. See Metzger, *A Textual Commen-tary on the Greek NT*, London/New York 1971, 725–6; M. Black, 'Critical and Exegetical Notes on Three New Testament Texts' in *Apophoreta*. Festschrift für E. Haenchen, Berlin 1964 39–45 (45); and C. D. Osburn, 'The Text of Jude 5', *Bib* 62 (1981) 107–15 (112, 115), now expanded in his 'Discourse Analysis and Jewish Apocalyptic in Jude', in: D. A. Black (ed.), *Linguistics and New Testament Interpreta-tion*, Nashville 1992, 295.

Probably, on balance, the reading 'Lord'[17] is to be preferred, meaning Yahweh, but brought into association with the work of Jesus who as the 'angel of the Lord'[18] executes the divine sentence. The connection with 4 is strong, and it is Jude's paradox that the one whom the teachers disown as Sovereign and Lord will appear as their judge just as he brought God's righteous sentence on the unbelieving Israelites in the wilderness. 'Lord' is Jude's favourite title for Jesus (4, 21, 25) along with a typically Jewish Christian affirmation of his messiahship. The designation 'only sovereign' in 4 is meant to rank Jesus on a par with God the Father who also is given the same title 'only' in 25. Both titles have a polemical thrust, calculated to stress that sole lordship and authority for moral standards reside only in the divine way, not worldly instincts (10).

Judgement, moreover, is certain, even if its timing lies in the future. Jude uses past examples to indicate that God's holy ways are sure. The past fate of Israel's unbelievers and the doom meted out to rebellious angels prove to Jude that God's judgements are to be taken seriously. And these examples point forward to the future judgement that must inevitably follow. So at 14 the appeal to 1 Enoch 1. 9 is made to refer by a kind of *midrash pesher* (i.e. interpretative exegetical device)[19] to the teachers whose ungodly character (in 12–13) makes their fate certain. So in 14, 'Enoch ... prophesied of these [men] also, when he said, "See, the Lord has come with a great host of his holy ones, to execute judgment".'

In stark contrast, the agency of Jesus as judge is tempered by his quality of 'mercy' which is the ground of confidence of Jude's friends (21) and equally the source of optimism for them to display as they reach out to rescue the wanderers (23), even if the obdurate and wayward can only be left to God's mercy.

---

[17] The divine name abbreviated to $\overline{KC}$ (for *kyrios*), was variously transcribed as $\overline{\Theta C}$ (for *theos*); IC (for *Iesous*). The textual problems in 5b are well displayed in Reymond, *L'épître*, 161–2 who concludes that the best text should be translated: 'I want to remind you, you who already are fully apprised of it all, that the Lord saved his people'.

[18] So Jarl Fossum, 'Kyrios Jesus as the Angel of the Lord in Jude 5–7', *NTS* 33 (1987) 226–43.

[19] See E. E. Ellis, *Prophecy and Hermeneutic*; J. D. Charles, 'Jude's Use', 141.

The verb attached to 'the mercy of our Lord Jesus Christ', in
21 suggests a looking ahead to Christ's appearing and his role
as final assessor of human life at the last day. Then his judgements and mercy will come together (cf. Jas. 2. 13).

3. The nature of Christian living as Jude describes it, notably
at 20–1, is a bulwark against deviation and falling away. On
these verses one commentator has written that they form

the burning centre of the entire exhortation of Jude, and along with
the exhortation [they describe] his complete understanding of the
Christian life.[20]

This is well said, and may be shown to be the case by observing
the strategic use of the verbs employed. The heart of Jude's
encouragement and admonition lies in the call: 'keep yourselves in the love of God'. This is a practical summons for the
readers to attend to, matching the assurance given in 1 that
they are 'kept [safe] for Jesus Christ' (cf. NRSV). The twin
sides of Christian truth are here displayed, in line with Jude's
strong theocentric belief that God is in charge of his people's
destiny in all ages and has a final purpose in view, which is to
'keep [them] from stumbling and to make them stand without
blemish in the presence of his glory with rejoicing' (24). Yet
those same people are not to be negligent and wayward like
unbelieving Israel (5) or the unstable and gullible adherents
(22–3). The danger that threatens in the alien teaching should
awaken them to their peril and alert them to their responsibility, which is to stay within the orbit of divine love and not
stray into ruin, as warning examples illustrate (11).

The practical means of their remaining 'safe' are then
spelled out by three link-verbs: 'building yourselves up in your
most holy faith, praying in the Holy Spirit, and expecting the
mercy of our Lord Jesus Christ, leading to eternal life' (21).
The syntactical arrangement suggests an intimate connection
and emphasizes the human endeavour needed to ensure divine
protection. The characteristic traits of Jude's understanding of
Christian living are here on display and embrace both a
confessional and a charismatic element. The 'most holy faith'

[20] Reymond, *L'épître*, 182.

looks back to the military call of 3, 'to fight for the faith' of apostolic integrity,[21] and not to be seduced into compromise, especially one that would lead to a moral disaster (4). The prayer-call echoes Paul's writing on the role of the Spirit as one who authenticates and informs Christian praying (Rom. 8. 26–7; cf. Eph. 6. 18) and places prayer under the charismatic banner. Likewise the verb 'expecting' orients faith to the future, and reminds the readers of the 'not-yet' dimension of their common salvation (3) which only the parousia of Jesus will bring to fulfilment in eternal life (in contrast to the 'eternal fire' awaiting the immoral, 7, and the 'eternal chains' by which the fallen angels are bound, 6).

The magnificent doxology (24–5) which rounds off the letter gathers into a closing tribute much of the hortatory and reassuring language. It is no surprise that Jude's letter is famed, where it is appraised at all, for this doxological encomium, and that these verses have found a place in liturgical service-books and worship manuals.

With close links to Rom. 16.27 (probably a redactional addition), 1 Tim. 1. 17; 6. 15–6, and maybe John 17.3, the final tribute to 'God only wise' recalls the Jewish confession in the *shema* (Deut. 6. 4) of Israel's sole deity. At the same time it associates God's saving power with 'Jesus Christ our Lord' – a Christian formulation that picks up the polemical exposure in 4.

The doxology makes a double statement. It is a recognition of God's action on behalf of believers (24); and it lifts up certain qualities of divine attributes (25). There is thus an exquisite blend of the subjective and the objective. In the latter class God's power is lauded with a fulsome piling up of attributes and characteristics, betraying the idiom of liturgy which is impressionistic and evocative. The ascription of praise is tailored to meet the subjective needs of the readers, while mixed metaphors that are confusing, if inspected logically, are set cheek-by-jowl. The readers are reminded finally of their

---

[21] See W. Grundmann, Excursus I, *Der Brief des Judas* Theologischer Handkommentar 15 (Berlin 1974), 'Zum Glaubensverständnis des Judasbriefes', 26f.

perilous state and ever-present need to be guarded from stumbling into error (11). At the same time they are assured that God's power is available to prevent this. Rather, that power will cause them to be steady and to stand at length as both blameless sacrifices at the temple altar and joyful worshippers ready to appear before the divine presence. Their joy is both cultic and eschatological. The first joy leads to the second (Ps. 50. 8, 12; 126. 5–6; Isa. 12. 6; 25. 9; 1 Pet. 1. 8; 4. 13; Rev. 19. 7). The single point to be made is that God's protection will bring the loyal readers – such is Jude's optimism – to their appointed destiny, in direct contrast to the fearful fate in store for the apostate and ungodly. The joyous reward for fidelity underlines Jude's essentially personal and pastoral motives; and his confidence in his readers' loyalty to the faith (3) is mellowed by his tribute that 'to be a believer is to keep oneself within God's love'.[22]

JUDE'S AFTER-LIFE: WINDOW AND MIRROR

What is the present-day reader to make of this brief but tantalizingly puzzling letter? 'Jude the obscure' is a true assessment.

Its harsh tones and bitter invective give the first impression of an author who is on edge and is cross with his opponents. Yet he can be tender and concerned about his implied readers whom he repeatedly calls 'dear people' (5, 17, 20), but in no unctuous, patronizing way that we associate with a pulpit announcement. Moreover, there are attractive features in his writing (1, 20–1, 24–5)[23] to the addressees, as well as a solicitude expressed for the wayward and unsteady church members (22–3). They are still his charge, and he offers practical steps to help their recovery.

Yet, on balance, this is 'a neglected letter' (to use Luther's

---

22 Reymond, *L'épître*, 182.
23 Origen remarks that 'Jude, who wrote an epistle of only a few lines, yet filled with healthful words of heavenly grace, said in the salutation': 1 is cited. See B. M. Metzger, *The Canon of the New Testament*, Oxford 1987, 138–9.

description[24]) that has lived for the most part of Christian history in the shadows; and only in the past century has it emerged as a distinctive part of the NT canon with a theological bent to give it a right to be read and heeded.

The moment we inquire about its theological setting we run into a big problem. If only we could set the letter in some historical, cultural, and social framework, our task would be easier; but, alas, the diversity of opinion about Jude's identity, circumstances, background, and method of writing is altogether bewildering. Options range from the traditional view that identifies Jude as the Lord's brother and a spokesperson for early Jewish Christianity[25] to a second-century dating that makes Jude a fictional name to give weight to an anonymous tract on behalf of early Catholic Christianity against gnosticizing deviance from the church's teaching.[26] On the literary front we are faced with proposals that Jude's epistle is simply an outpouring of venom in a disorderly fashion to being a carefully constructed piece of rhetoric set in an artificial epistolary frame that conceals its well-ordered flow of *narratio* (4), *probatio* (5–16) to *peroratio* (17–23) – all of which 'conform to [the] best principles' of Graeco-Roman rhetoric.[27] The main emphasis is on methods of proof from past examples and applications to the present needs of his readers whom he wishes to win over by argumentation, use of authoritative sources, and deliberative appeal and constraint. On the latter view Jude has

---

[24] Preface to *Episteln S. Jacobi und Judas* (1545). He offers the reason that Jude is dependent on, and contained in, 2 Peter. Luther is followed by the European Reformers who dismissed Jude as deutero-canonical (Metzger, *Canon of the New Testament*, 244). Cf. the title of D.J. Rowston's study 'The Most Neglected Book in the New Testament', *NTS* 21 (1974–5) 554–63, with some reasons for its neglect, especially its use of the pseudepigraphical book of Enoch (Jerome calls it 'apocryphal') and our lack of knowledge of a particular historical situation.

[25] Especially argued for by Bauckham (note 2) and his *Commentary*, 14–16.

[26] So E. Käsemann, 'An Apologia for Primitive Christian Eschatology', *Essays on New Testament Themes*, London 1964.

[27] D. F. Watson, *Invention, Arrangement, and Style*. Rhetorical Criticism of Jude and 2 Peter. SBLDS 104, Atlanta 1988, 78; J. D. Charles, 'Literary Artifice in the Epistle of Jude', *ZNW* 82 (1991) 106–24 for ample evidence of 'a literary-rhetorical artist at work' (124); and for conceptual links in an elaborately constructed treatise, see Charles, '"Those" and "These" in the Use of the Old Testament in the Epistle of Jude', *JSNT* 38 (1990) 109–24.

much to contribute as a paradigm of early Christian techniques of invention and persuasion.

Of more immediate interest is the suggestion that we should first approach Jude as a window through which we look in the hope of seeing the type of Christian community it addressed.[28] In an earlier discussion we have sought to identify certain traits of this congregation. Let us review briefly.

The addressees were threatened by itinerant intruders who offered a blend of sophistication and immediacy. They claimed (Jude is reporting, perhaps overzealously) to be super-spiritual, to be beyond the reach of morality, probably with no fear of judgement to come, to recognize no divine authority save their access to the divine (and so they paid no regard to the angels), and to be a financial liability on the community. Jude seeks to expose by painting them and their practices in lurid colours and then to rebut (implicit) beliefs and behaviour. If we are searching for a conceivable historical parallel, it will be the situation reflected in Didache chs. 11–13. There itinerant and ecstatic prophets and missionaries are moving into the area of Syria-Palestine (around *c.* 80 CE) making claims for extended hospitality and seeking financial gains, and exerting their influence, especially at the agape meal table. The Didachist enters a firm warning and level-headed caution against such people, appealing to the office of bishops and deacons (15. 1) and making the apostolic gospel the depository of authority, with constant recourse to 'the gospel' (Did. 8. 2; 11. 3; 15. 3–4) and the 'ways of the Lord' (1. 1; 4. 14; 11. 8) against a strongly worded apocalyptic backdrop (Did. 16). Points of comparison between Jude and the Didache are not far to seek, and the two documents illumine each other as a window into first-century Jewish Christianity as it moved to a more settled, authoritatively based hierarchy of leaders connected with the Holy Family against the more free-wheeling, charismatically inspired prophetic movement that, from the standpoint of the Didache, is on the way out. Jude's

---

[28] The analogies of window and mirror, as well as a text's *Nachleben* or After-life, are now commonly used in literary criticism of the NT. For the former, see S. D. Moore, *Literary Criticism and the Gospels*, New Haven/London 1989, 19–20.

appeal to apostolic norms (3, 17, 20) of belief and conduct incorporates apocalyptic ideas[29] to enforce judgement on evil persons who are accused of leading immoral lives (a standard allegation). Charismatic inspiration needs the control of church authority based on apostolic precedent and witness just as Enoch's apocalyptic tirade (14) is turned against the teachers who may have held the writings of Enoch in high regard.[30]

As we utilize Jude more as a mirror, it becomes an exercise of some conjecture and suggestiveness to see what the text may reflect back to the modern reader. This is part of the discipline of reader-response whereby the ancient text becomes opaque and provides a looking-glass in which we perceive ourselves as much as the real and implied author and readers.

True, each present-day reader will bring his or her own individuality to a text like Jude, if we have patience to enter sympathetically into the (reconstructed) scene and open ourselves to some kind of 'personal transaction' (Norman Holland's term) with the text. We might then gain the impression of a church assembly divided over how ancient scriptures are to be viewed, where authority is to be located, whether in immediate experience (charismatic) or traditional power bases (Holy Family, apostolic order, and teaching), and the role played by past examples, warnings, and incentives. As we saw earlier, the church's life, as far as we can discern it from this brief letter, is more like the charismatic, spontaneous, and unfettered ways of 1 Cor. and the Acts of the Apostles than the more rigid and formal patterns in the apostolic fathers. Jude's appeal looks to this presentation of church 'order' in which the

---

[29] This is now commonplace in recent studies of the letter, e.g. various literary and stylistic symbolisms 'allow one to classify the book as Jewish Christian apocalyptic' (Rowston, 'The Most Neglected Book', 561).

[30] This insight permits Charles ('Judes' Use', 143–4) to claim that the citation in Jude 14–15 is introduced by a translation, 'For even (your own) Enoch, the seventh from Adam, prophesied of these, saying', which suggests that Jude has adapted the Enoch quotation for his own theological and literary ends. So the use of a pseudepigraphical source is more an acknowledgment of others' high regard for Enoch than an admission, on Jude's part, that it is authoritative – a quality he gives only to the OT canonical books (5, 7, 11) and authoritative apostolic teaching, i.e. the 'received' traditions of 3, 17. See now Charles' book *Literary Strategy in the Epistle of Jude*, Scranton 1993.

members are encouraged to search the scriptures for themselves (like the Bereans of Acts 17. 10–12) and enjoy the Spirit's
freedom (20). Yet as Paul found at Corinth, there need to be
controls and safeguards (1 Cor. 14. 33–40) which he found in
the claims of the church as a unity, held together by love and
guided by a concern to build up one's neighbour. Jude meets a
situation where immediate inspiration is claimed, and offers his
controls in his appeals to unity (19) and a common faith (3) as
well as the church's rootage in a history that goes back to the
Lord and his apostles (17).

The issues posed here are still with us today, just as they
continued to surface throughout church history. The compet-
ing claims of those who look for validation of their religious
experience no farther than in their own inner illumination and
certainty will be in tension with those of other Christians who
find strength in institutional forms and structures: the creeds,
the historic church and its accredited leaders, tradition, and
continuity with the past – these are their grounds of confidence.

At first sight the two claims seem mutually exclusive, and to
maintain one viewpoint is evidently to cancel out or deny the
other. But only at first sight. Deeper reflection may lead us to
believe that we need both in complementary fashion.

Christianity is always 'an affair of the heart', evoking our
love for God and neighbour (and enemy!) as God has loved us
and blessed us in Christ who is both the sign of that divine love
and the focus of our responding love. To that extent the
definition of Christianity as 'the life of God in the souls of men'
and women is sound. Yet it is a definition crying out for
expression in tangible and measurable 'forms', in the realities
of social life and communal existence. That is why the church,
with its scriptures, its faith, and its appeal to the past, is part of
our heritage, as it was of Jude's message in his day.

Two salient matters stay in the mind as we rise from this
exercise of mirror-gazing. First, for Jude morality is a strenuous
and serious business. If his method of rough-handling and
browbeating the opposition with dire threats cannot be ours, it
still remains the case that 'grace' can be perverted and the road

to cheap and easy salvation with no moral claims laid upon us is an ever-present false trail in all generations. The seductions of those who offer a 'quick fix' salvation are met by the stringent ethic reflected in this letter, with its reminder that the moral undergirding of the religious life can never safely be relaxed.

Second, the recall of the past examples Jude employs as a literary and homiletical device may lack some cogency today. And the apparent acceptance of 1 Enoch as authoritative scripture may raise problems with some modern readers. The citation of a non-canonical authority, 1 Enoch in 14–15 is a rare case in the New Testament, though it may fairly be claimed that such an appeal to a pseudonymous book is Jude's strategy to use a source that was venerated by his opponents and so to gain an advantage over them, much like Paul's appeal to a Greek poet at Areopagus (Acts 17. 28). Yet both Jude and Paul do seem to regard their non-canonical sources as authoritative and as expressing Christian truth. Perhaps we need to enlarge our vision of the truth to take in those insights that the biblical writers and speakers thought it worthwhile and significant to include.

A more problematic question is whether the calling up of past historical illustrations as Jude habitually does can have the same probative force today as he apparently expected. The past is not always our wisest teacher, but we neglect it at our cost. Moreover, in the biblical tradition of both testaments, the past is never thought of as 'dead', beyond recall and forgotten. Jude's illustrative material ranges from the traditional and hackneyed (for example, Sodom and Gomorrah as chiefest sinners) to the esoteric and bizarre (the mythological account in Gen. 6 and the apocalyptic scenario of the angels' fall). But the past is all we have to form our heritage and influence; and it is a helpful observation that

The past is ... a reservoir of meaning available for those with memory ... The past is present not only as yielding a moral significance, warning of dangers which threaten, but also as a key to understand the present.[31]

---

[31] Reymond, *L'épître*, 163.

CHAPTER 6

1 Peter

ONE

INTRODUCING 1 PETER

1 Peter is a New Testament letter which church tradition has classified as 'catholic', meaning universal. In its original sense the term suggests a collection of documents intended for wide distribution throughout the Christian world. In the case of 1 Peter, however, the designation catholic is less appropriate, since the definite geographical area of the first recipients is given (1. 1). The readers are referred to throughout as a well-defined group of Christian congregations, often addressed in terms of endearment (2. 11; 4. 12), facing a set of specific circumstances, and marked off from the rest of Christendom scattered throughout the ancient Mediterranean world (5. 9).

The first readers lived in the north-east section of Asia, modern Turkey, distributed in provinces, two of which bordered on each other and were called Bithynia and Pontus (1. 1: the orders of names is not haphazard, but follows the sequence of a courier's travels in the system of letter-carriers (*grammatophoroi*) used by wealthy merchants, commencing from Amisus in Pontus and terminating in adjacent Bithynia[1]). The same readers in this region well away from the centres of Roman civilization and culture were mainly Gentiles. We read of their former way of life in the throes of the evils around them – seen from a Jewish point of view with its high-toned morality and

---

[1] See C. J. Hemer, 'The Address of 1 Peter', *ExpT* 89 (1977–8) 239–43.

sense of self-restraint (1. 18; 4. 3–4). Yet the author expects them to be familiar with the Old Testament by, for instance, making much of the annual service of redemption and remembrance called Passover (1. 18–19).

The books of the Old Testament are constantly quoted in the author's appeal, especially Isaiah 53 (in 2. 21–25) and Psalm 34 (quoted in 3. 10–12). One recent study has insisted that 1 Peter is to be read as an extensive example of interpretative commentary on the OT, called homiletical midrash. W. L. Schutter[2] argues that nearly one half of the letter is OT material, including forty-six quotations and pointers as well as allusions, especially allusions to Ezekiel chs. 8–11. Whether this is an accurate assessment or not, it remains the case that *no NT book* (with the possible exception of Romans and Hebrews) *is so permeated with OT hints and ideas* as well as actual citations as 1 Peter; and that fact has some bearing on the type of document it is and the kind of readers who would be in a position to follow and appreciate this sort of sustained biblical exposition and application.

The readers' situation was evidently unenviable. They were undergoing trials (1. 6) and testings (4. 12). The chief reason for the letter is directly related to this need – to encourage the harassed believers to stand firm in God's grace (5. 12). The letter is essentially one of encouragement in the dual sense of calling on those in the face of their present troubles both to bear up under trial and to cheer up when their spirits are down. The notes of sympathy and a close bond between author and readers are sounded repeatedly. If this is a letter intended for a wide constituency scattered over a considerable area, it is at the same time remarkably personal and understanding of the readers' needs, and breathes a spirit of fellow-feeling and solicitude for them in their present lot. See, for instance, 1. 6–9; 1. 22; 3. 13; 4. 7–11; 5. 1–2; 5. 14.

Peter's basis for this exhortation is hope, itself based on the resurrection of Jesus. Paul's usual word for one's response to God's love seen in the resurrection is faith, but, for Peter, the

---

[2] W. L. Schutter, *Hermeneutic and Composition in 1 Peter*, Tübingen 1989, 35–43.

two terms, hope and faith, overlap (1. 21). The letter concentrates on hope as the incentive needed to carry them through their trials to hope's ultimate reward (1. 3, 8, 13; 3. 5, 15; 5. 10).

The Christian message was brought to the readers by evangelists sent out to their provinces (1. 10–12). The author evidently does not know his audience at first hand, and, in 1. 8–9, he puts a distance between them and himself. He has some eyewitness knowledge of the Lord (5. 1); they are not so privileged. *The leading idea running through the entire letter is found just here.* By a common participation in the messianic blessing realized in Christ and the new age and through a shared study of ancient scriptures, both first generation Christians (represented by Peter the apostle at the fountainhead) and any subsequent generation of responsive believers stand together as on the same ground. Perhaps it is this conviction that gives to 1 Peter its timeless appeal and Christian character as a witness-bearing document. It invites us to look at it as binding together Christians in varying circumstances, different cultures, and diverse backgrounds as those who, with access to Christ mediated through the scriptures, discover his contemporary presence, and find in him God's strength to help in time of social adjustment, painful acculturation, and religious change.

At this juncture three pressure points in the readers' needs may be mentioned. First, they were at odds with society around them and feeling the sharp pricks of 'persecution' from local officials and community pressures (1. 6; 3. 13–14; 4. 4, 12–16; 5. 9–10). Then, their social status was thrown into question by their acceptance of a new religion, and at least some of the letter reflects the felt need of an alienated social group whose underpinnings have been swept away as a direct consequence of their conversion to Christianity (2. 10; 4. 4). Third, and at the theological level, as new believers they were wrestling with some age-old issues, Why do good people suffer? Why does God allow trials to happen? Where, in fact, is God in all the uncertainties and contrarieties of life when opposition breaks upon believers for no reason? See 1. 6; 2. 19; 4. 12.

1 Peter's response is spelled out along these three same lines.

In the first place, the readers' attractive conduct is the best answer to hostile neighbours and the authorities (2. 12, 16–17; 3. 16; 4. 12–16). Then, the social identity they fear to be lost is replaced by a new sense of belonging to the 'people of God', stretching back to Abraham and Sarah (3. 5, 6) and onward to the complete 'household of faith' one day to be realized (2. 4–10; 4. 17–19). Finally, 1 Peter's main contribution to the theology of suffering is its recourse to theodicy, which is an attempt to explain how God's plan is at work in and through human pain, misery, and affliction. At the end of history this plan will be fully known (1. 5–9; 4. 7; 5. 10).

Here, then, is a ground plan of what 1 Peter has to offer. Inasmuch as the three issues mentioned are still relevant in several parts of the world to which the Christian gospel is introduced as a provocation to resistance, a disturbance within the social order, and a heightening of tension about the divine character, it may have a far-reaching appeal.

In that sense 1 Peter is a truly 'catholic' epistle.

SOME BACKGROUND DATA

A whole range of historical, critical, and exegetical questions is covered by this heading. It will only be feasible to mention a few of the solutions proposed, and that more by way of summary statements of options and possibilities.

Three basic positions have been adopted to explain the *origin* of 1 Peter: (1) direct authorship by the apostle Peter, a leader in the Jerusalem Church known mainly from the record in Acts chs. 1–12 and Galatians; (2) indirect Petrine authorship through an amanuensis Silvanus (as a scribe or as a secretary who worked with creative freedom), and (3) pseudonymous authorship by someone of the Petrine circle, who used the master's name to perpetuate his memory and teaching.

1 Peter: a community product?

Some biblical scholars have concluded that neither Peter nor an amanuensis contemporary with Peter could have produced

1 Peter. The earliest statement of this idea was that of the Tübingen School. They viewed the letter as a later celebration of the union between rival Pauline and Petrine parties, accounting for the Pauline elements under a Petrine pseudonym. While such a motivation for pseudonymity has been abandoned today, the theory of pseudonymity has been retained. This theory has been explained by a variety of motivations. Conclusions about pseudonymity in general remain unresolved and complicate this discussion. Several modern scholars are unhappy with the notion that early Christian groups would deliberately add the name of an apostle to a piece of writing and pass it off as the apostle's own work. But no such intention to deceive seems implied in this procedure of using the name of a great Christian leader, especially after that person's faithful life and martyr's death. In so attributing a writing to an apostle, the early church was affirming the leader's abiding presence and valuing the legacy of his continuing influence. In this way they were appealing to what the apostle might have said if he had survived to a later decade. It is only a short step to conclude that the apostle's spirit lives on in the experience of his followers, because he is thought to be alive in God's presence.

So a development of the theory of pseudonymity is the proposal of the existence of a Petrine school located in Rome which is responsible for the production of 1 Peter.[3] A Petrine community is described by four observations:

First, the similarities and dissimilarities in 1 Peter, 2 Peter, and Jude could best be explained by community authorship. Second, the liturgical elements in these three letters would point to a worshipping community. Third, the unique use of Old Testament, dominical logia, early church traditions, and pseudepigraphical literature involves a community design. Fourth, evidence within the New Testament and church fathers gives that indication.[4]

A more specific statement of the proposal of a Petrine school is the identification of Silvanus, Mark, and the 'co-elect sister in Babylon' referred to in 5. 13 where 'Babylon' is a cryptogram for Rome as the collective authors of 1 Peter.

[3] See Marion L. Soards's contribution to *ANRW* 2/25, section 5, (1985), 3827–49.
[4] J. L. Blevins, 'Introduction to 1 Peter', *Review and Expositor* 79 (1982) 402.

The question of authorship remains unresolved. Given the state of the art and the tentative nature of the science of the critical methods applied to this question, any dogmatic assertions proclaiming certainty are inappropriate. F. W. Beare's conclusion[5] that 'there can be no possible doubt that "Peter" is a pseudonym' can be attributed to the overconfidence of early critical conclusions. D. Guthrie's[6] opposing conclusion of 'no doubt that the traditional view which accepts the claims of the epistle to be apostolic is more reasonable than any alternative hypothesis' is premature, as there remains some uncertainty among even conservative scholars, such as Michaels, Davids, and Marshall.[7]

While the question of the authorship of 1 Peter must remain open, the internal claims to Peter as author are rightly referred to as a primary evidence. The external evidence of its acceptance as produced by Peter is also of major value in determining the origin of the epistle. The onus of proving otherwise is on those who reject the traditional position. Yet the insight that a document like 1 Peter may well be the final product of a group associated with Peter in his lifetime and intent on publishing his teaching after his demise is gaining ground, and holds out the most promise for future understanding.[8]

It is obvious in the above discussion on authorship that the question of *dating* is a closely related issue. If Peter is accepted as the author of 1 Peter, or an amanuensis working with Peter, then the document is to be placed in the 60s CE, probably during Nero's emperorship. The pseudonymous theory was originally presented as requiring a late date (90s–111/12 CE)

---

[5] F. W. Beare, *The First Epistle of Peter*, 3rd edn., Oxford 1970, 44.

[6] D. Guthrie, *New Testament Introduction*, 3rd edn., London 1970, 790.

[7] J. R. Michaels, *1 Peter*, WBC 49, Waco 1988; P. H. Davids, *The First Epistle of Peter*, Grand Rapids 1990; I. H. Marshall, *1 Peter*, Leicester 1991, 21–4, who finally comes down on the side of Petrine authorship.

[8] See in particular *Peter in the New Testament*, eds. R. E. Brown, K. P. Donfried, and J. Reumann, Minneapolis 1973, ch. 9; J. H. Elliott, *A Home for the Homeless*, Philadelphia/London, 1981, and 'Peter, Silvanus and Mark in 1 Peter and Acts', in W. Haubeck and M. Bachmann (eds.), *Wort in der Zeit*, Leiden 1980, 250–67; M. L. Soards, '1 Peter, 2 Peter, and Jude as Evidence for a Petrine School', *ANRW* 2/25, section 5, 3827–49.

which was a response to other evidence as described earlier. An intermediate view, put out by Michaels,[9] that the author is Peter who survived the Neronian pogrom and lived on into a later decade when he wrote the letters, is not likely to gain wide acceptance, since it defies all the best evidence available regarding Peter's demise in 65 CE.

Several other considerations mark the discussion of date. First, the code word 'Babylon' (5. 13) is not usually found prior to the destruction of Jerusalem in 70 CE. Such usage is expressed by the Book of Revelation which is generally dated 95 CE or later.[10] However, the designation could have been used of Rome in the 60s after Nero's persecution. A lot turns on the use of 'Babylon' as a cipher in 5. 13. It is obviously a cryptic term designed to conceal as much as to reveal. The usual view is to see it as functioning symbolically as in the Apocalypse where it hides the politically dangerous belief that imperial Rome is to be overthrown (Rev. 18. 1–24).

But certain differences in the ethos of the two documents are to be noted. In Revelation, 'Babylon' carries all manner of sinister associations as Mother of Prostitutes and of the Abominations of the Earth (Rev. 17. 5). This is hardly the tenor of 1 Peter, where the government is much more the servant of God, akin to Paul's teaching in Romans 13. 1–10. The Petrine attitude (2. 16–17) is one of respect and obedience, not violent hatred and subversion.

This dissonance between two uses of a common symbol in two NT books has led to a more promising idea: that Babylon is a cipher of the exile of God's people whether on the analogy of Israel's captivity in Mesopotamian Babylonia in the sixth century BCE (Moule[11]) or as the counterpoint to Peter's teaching on the church as residing in the Diaspora as pilgrims and

---

[9] J. R. Michaels, *1 Peter*, WBC 49, Waco, 1988, lxi–lxvii.
[10] C.-H. Hunzinger, 'Babylon als Deckname für Rom und die Datierung des 1 Petrusbriefes', in: *Gottes Word und Gottes Land*. Festschrift für H.-W. Hertzberg, (ed.) H. Reventlow Göttingen 1965 67–77, who emphasized the apocalyptic character of the name for Rome.
[11] C. F. D. Moule, 'The Nature and Purpose of 1 Peter', *NTS* 3 (1956–7), 1–11.

exiles (as in 1. 1; 2. 11). Yet again it has been suggested[12] that as one of the leading motifs of 1 Peter is redemption based on Israel's need and experience according to Deutero-Isaiah (Isa. 48. 20; 51. 11; 52. 7–12) so Babylon is a suitable code-term for the place of Christian exile promising liberation from bondage to freedom in the Zion of the Christian community (1 Pet. 2. 1–10).

Second, the content of 1 Peter (especially 5. 9) evidences the existence of Christianity as widespread. (While this consideration is not conclusive it is part of the evidence that has been considered.)

Another approach to dating 1 Peter has come from form-critical studies which examine the use of early traditions as in this letter as compared to their use in other works. Such studies are based on a theory of the development of original forms in particular directions. For example, 1 Peter 3. 18–21 in its original format may be seen as a rudimentary version of the more elaborated Christological saga in 1 Timothy 3. 16. And the 'servant of God' pattern in 1 Peter 2. 18–24 represents a kind of early Christology that quickly dropped out from developing Christian thought. Conclusions from such study recognize the primitive nature of 1 Peter.[13] Serious questions are being asked of this theory of the development of forms, however, and methodological uncertainties plague discussion along these lines.

Accepting as a working hypothesis the origin of 1 Peter in a group of Peter's associates in the decade or so after his martyrdom, we may place its appearance in the time frame of 75–85 CE.[14]

---

[12] Here I recognize the unpublished work of my research student Sharon Clark Pearson.

[13] This is Selwyn's conclusion in his pioneering study, *The First Epistle of St. Peter*, London 1946; see too P. E. Davies, 'Primitive Christology in 1 Peter', in: E. H. Barth and R. E. Cocroft (eds.), *Festschrift to Honor F. Wilbur Gingrich*, Leiden 1972, 115–22.

[14] See the bibliographical data displayed in E. Cothenet, 'La Première de Pierre: bilan de 35 ans de recherches', *ANRW* 2/25, section 5, 3686–711; D. Sylva, in: C. H. Talbert (ed.), *Perspectives on 1 Peter*, Macon 1986, ch. 2; 'A 1 Peter Bibliography' *JETS* 25/1 (1982) 75–89; and '1 Peter Studies: The State of the Discipline', *BTB* 10 (1980) 155–63.

THE COMPOSITION OF I PETER

Once more we are faced with a wide variety of options in responding to the question which on face value is a simple and straightforward one. What kind of a document is 1 Peter? What of its literary or rhetoric form or genre? Assuming that the document as it now appears in the NT is cast in epistolary form, with author, addressees, and closing greeting – all marks of letter-writing style – could it be that 1 Peter is really another sort of literary piece dressed up in epistolary clothes?

Traditionally the document has been taken as a letter, even if it may incorporate fragments of hymns, creeds, confessions, and hortatory, homiletical, and expository materials alongside its frequent recourse to the OT. This common-sense view may appeal to such references as 5. 12: 'I have written this short letter to encourage you . . .' (NRSV).

No fewer than three separate possibilities as to the original format of 1 Peter have been ventilated, each deserving a brief mention.

(a) As *a baptismal address* 1 Peter was classified as such mainly as a result of applying form-critical techniques to the NT letters. Scholars identified a number of Christological hymns in a baptismal setting, even suggesting that separate verses could be linked together to form a consecutive creed handed over to new converts at their baptism, for example, 1.20 + 2. 18–25 + 3. 18–22.[15] Yet one of the main pieces of evidence was the detecting of a 'break' after the doxology of 4. 11, thus creating the theory of two separate documents (1. 3–4. 11; 4. 12–5 11) now stitched together in our 1 Peter. It was first thought that 1. 3–4. 11 was the genuine core, followed by 4. 12–5. 11 which confronted a more ominous situation in which trials are present and more threatening. (This partitioning of the letter will be discussed later.) The character of

---

[15] R. Deichgräber, *Gotteshymnus und Christushymnus in der frühen Christenheit*, Göttingen 1967, 169–73, specially in reference to R. Bultmann, 'Bekenntnis – und Liedfragmente im ersten Petrusbrief', *Coniectanea Neotestamentica* 11 Lund, 1947 1–14 (reprinted in Bultmann's *Exegetica*, ed. E. Dinkler, Tübingen 1967, 285–97). See the survey in R. P. Martin, *New Testament Foundations*, vol. 2, 2nd edn., Grand Rapids, 1978, 335–44.

1. 3–4. 11 is that of a baptismal homily directed to new converts at the point of their initiation (described in the hiatus between 1. 21 and 1. 22) into the Christian family and fellowship.

Linked with this imaginative reconstruction is the even more daring scenario that 1 Peter is 'the transcript of an actual baptismal service in progress'[16] or even the document as a service-book depicting the celebrant's part in the Easter Paschal baptismal service.[17]

Recent investigation has poured a douse of cold water on much of this theorizing, not least with the simple reminder that 'baptism' is a term that occurs only once in the entire writing of 1 Peter (3. 21).

(b) The word-group that does feature prominently in the entire letter – and with no appreciable shift of meaning in the two hypothetical halves – is suffer/suffering (found eleven times of the verb; four times of the noun). A clue to 1 Peter may well lie here; it is *an apologetic tract* offered to explain the readers' trials and so to enhearten them.[18] The case of slaves would naturally be a tender spot for the author's concern, as slaves were a marginalized class open to maltreatment and abuse (so 2. 18–25). Yet the suffering is much wider than that, and Peter's attention is directed to the entire Christian community in Roman Asia (1. 1) and beyond (5. 9–10).

Those who view 1 Peter as aimed at a target audience of a persecuted church move on to consider the nature of these trials. They not only arise from the Christian identity of the readers, but focus on the very nature of Christian existence in society (as Goppelt was the first to plot[19]) and more particularly because the Christian household was the paradigm of how believers were beginning to view themselves self-consciously

---

[16] Cf. H. Preisker, in his supplement to H. Windisch, *Die katholischen Briefe*, HNT, Tübingen 1951, 157: 'ein urchristlicher Gottesdienst einer Taufgemeinde'.

[17] F. L. Cross, *1 Peter: A Paschal Liturgy*, London 1954.

[18] E. Lohse in his essay, 'Parenesis and Kerygma in 1 Peter' in: C. H. Talbert (ed.), *Perspectives on First Peter*, Macon, GA, 1986, 37–59, makes this a leading theme of the letter. See too D. Hill, 'On Suffering and Baptism in 1 Peter', *NovT* 18 (1976) 181–9.

[19] L. Goppelt, *Der erste Petrusbrief*, ed. F. Hahn, Meyerk 12/1 Göttingen, 1978.

as part of social adjustment and accepting new loyalties. J. H. Elliott[20] made the point of 1 Peter's addressing a set of Christian social groups feeling dislocated and bereft once the old ties had been severed or strained. He reconstructs the background of the letter in a set of social conflicts which ranged the readers as poor, rural dwellers against the urban culture of the rich cities of Asia. The latter typifies the evil world against which the church struggles to maintain an identity as the 'household of God', self-contained yet stricken with an acute sense of rootlessness and a feeling of not-belonging. Elliott sees the controlling metaphor in 1 Peter to be the 'household' or 'family' of God understood more in a sociological than a religious way. The readers' calling as 'resident aliens' (1. 17; 2. 11) speaks of their social status prior to their conversion, as well as to their place on the socio-economic ladder. It is a token of their social rank more than their religious identity – a point that is open to the criticism that Peter is surely more concerned to stress theological than sociological changes (see later, p. 100). In any case, the two markers clearly overlap. It is not difficult to see modern parallels in Latin American countries and among Christian believers in some African republics.

D. L. Balch[21] took a more positive line in seeing apologetical value as belonging to 1 Peter's bid to acculturate Christianity to Graeco-Roman family life, making much of the domestic code in 2. 13–3. 18. The thrust of the letter, he avers, is to demonstrate how Christians can co-exist in the empire as good citizens. The warning notes of 'Don't conform' are muted in Balch's presentation, and for this omission and neglected emphasis he too has been criticized (see later p. 127).

(c) Yet one other attempt to give a rationale to the forms incorporated in 1 Peter emerges from the study of the OT in the epistle. W. L. Schutter[22] argues that by a comparative study of hermeneutical methods found in 1 Peter it is feasible

---

[20] J. H. Elliott, *A Home for the Homeless. A Sociological Exegesis of 1 Peter. Its Situation and Strategy*, London/Philadelphia 1982.

[21] D. L. Balch, *Let Wives be Submissive. The Domestic Code in 1 Peter*, Chico 1981. See too his essay and that of Elliott in: C. H. Talbert (ed.), *Perspectives on First Peter*, Macon 1986.

[22] W. L. Schutter, *Hermeneutic and Composition in 1 Peter*, Tübingen 1989.

that the author used a specialized technique (called homiletical midrash) to enforce the chief point that 1 Peter is all about
the church as the temple-community (in 2. 9–10; 2. 4–8; 3. 15–16;
4. 12–17) and is a bold venture in early Christian self-identifi-
cation, buttressed by a constant exposition of OT testimonies,
text-plots, and allusions. Schutter holds 1. 10–12 to be the key
to the entire epistle, and this scripture-appeal and investigative
procedure reveals the author's intent: to highlight the time of
eschatological fulfilment, based on the Christ-event, supported
by OT scripture and aided by an elaborate, if implicit, doctrine of the Spirit. He envisages the church of 1 Peter as a kind
of scripture study group patterned on the community of the
Dead Sea scrolls.

EVALUATIONS, AND A POINTER TO THE LETTER'S THEOLOGY

The traditional theory of the document as a genuine hortatory
epistle has withstood direct attack, and absorbed the findings
of form-, source-, and redaction-criticism. A growing consensus
supports the position that 1 Peter is a genuine epistle, and
affirms the literary coherence of the letter. The differences in
style in the letter are to be attributed to the various sources
(such as liturgical forms) employed and redacted and linked
with the concerns of the author(s). Whatever the rhetoric or
logic of the text is, its reception into the canon as a literary text
is the best indication of its character as an encyclical letter,[23]
sent out to an identifiable constituency in the name of a
well-known leader in early Christianity (1. 1; 5. 1, 12).

As for the theories that arose out of the appreciation of the
baptismal references and backgrounds – the actual term
baptism occurs only once at 3. 21 in the text of 1 Peter – the
evidence is too scarce to support a primary designation of the
document as a baptismal address. The traditional deposits
(whether liturgical or homiletical) in 1 Peter which indicate a

---

[23] L. Goppelt, *Der erste Petrusbrief*, 44–5 speaks of Peter as a *Rundbrief*, with examples
from 2 Macc. 1. 1–9; 1. 10–2. 18; Jer. 29. 4–23; syr. Bar. 78. 1–86. 2.

baptismal *Sitz im Leben* do not define the composition of the
letter. F. W. Beare's evaluation of the evidence in 1 Peter is a
helpful corrective to any such supposition:

> rather than the direct use of fragments of a liturgy, the evidence seems
> to me to indicate a sermon developed along lines suggested by the
> structure of the liturgy, perhaps with an occasional outright quo-
> tation of familiar credal formulas, but as a rule freely expressed in the
> writer's own words and style.[24]

The more extreme theory based on what are claimed as
baptismal materials, the baptismal liturgy theory, seems to
have been totally disproved in the ongoing discussion of the
nature of 1 Peter. That a baptismal liturgy could be lifted from
a church in one location (such as Rome) and placed, without
comment, in the framework of a letter to Christians in various
congregations in Asia Minor is hard to credit. The literary
features appealed to in support of this theory (such as changes
in verb tenses and recognition of distinct sections) are less
obvious and less significant than the theory has portrayed them
and can be explained by more reasonable alternatives. Best,
Dalton, and Goppelt, all from various vantage points, successfully defend the unity and coherence of the letter. W. J.
Dalton's method is particularly successful in demonstrating the
unity of the document.[25] It consists of analysis of the literary
techniques of the author, particularly the use of scripture as a
court of appeal.

It is the consistency of 1 Peter's recourse to OT testimonia
that gives strength to Schutter's thesis, but his work concerning
the social processes that gave birth to Peter's design in writing
to these Asian communities is vague.

Here – in acknowledgement of the sociological issue yet with
some caution – the apologetic motif comes into its own, and
points to the theological centre of 1 Peter's thought. The
valued work on the social, political, and economic conditions
that inferentially prevailed in the churches of 1. 1 will stand,

[24] F. W. Beare, *The First Epistle of Peter*, 3rd edn., Oxford 1970, 226.
[25] W. J. Dalton, *Christ's Proclamation to the Spirits. A Study of 1 Peter 3. 18–4. 6*, Rome
1965, 2nd edn., 1989.

needing to be augmented by still more valuable and accurate assessment (by Achtemeier[26]) that 1 Peter is above all a *theological–ecclesiological document* bent on demonstrating to a disenfranchised and alienated people that their real roots are in the people of God, of both covenant ages, and their heritage of faith and hope is the religious (and not simply social, as Elliott implies) antidote to the prevailing loss of identity. Achtemeier points to the link between the roots *paroikos/oikos* ('foreigner'/ 'house-household') and *parepidēmoi* (2. 11: 'foreigners and *strangers* in the world', NIV), and notes how in the Greek Bible they are joined (Gen. 23. 4; Ps. 38. 13 (39. 12)) to convey the idea of God's people set in a hostile world. It is significant that 2. 11 comes directly after the exposition of the church as the people of God in 2. 1–10, which suggests that the controlling metaphor throughout 1 Peter (extending from 1. 1 to 5. 9) is that of Christians as the new chosen people of God, called to find their true identity in a witness-bearing community living often in tension with the world and not conforming to its ethos (against Balch). The church is aided by the example of the suffering and exalted Lord in whose steps Christians are to walk now (2. 21) in hope of final vindication. The time span of what is true *now* (suffering) and what may be confidently expected *then* (reward) is at the heart of 1 Peter's religious advice and theological pattern, and is based on the model of the two-beat rhythm of Jesus' example of his suffering and vindication.

The disjunction we, in the Western world, make between the present and the future, in which the future is an objective to be planned and provided for, is not one shared in ancient society. For the ancients their 'forthcoming' future was already in some way present now. The transition in 1 Peter from a painful present to a glorious future is more easily recognizable than we

---

[26] P. J. Achtemeier, 'Newborn Babes and Living Stones: Literal and Figurative in 1 Peter', in: M. P. Horgan and P. J. Kobelski (eds.), *To Touch the Text*. Festschrift for J. A. Fitzmyer, New York 1989, 207–36. His thesis is that the 'controlling metaphor' in 1 Peter is 'the Christian community as the new people of God constituted by the Christ who suffered (and rose)' (224). To this remark may be added 'in triumph over his enemies and theirs' to include the idea of Christ's representative sufferings and victory.

may imagine, since the seeds of what is to come are here and now, and the future can be greeted as 'real', not imaginary or fanciful. This distinction, made in B. J. Malina's interesting discussion[27] holds a valuable key to Peter's close linkage of experience and hope.

In sum, 1 Peter stands as a genuinely epistolary work, yet incorporating putative hymnic, liturgical, and homiletical traditions borrowed from the worshipping life of the early Christian communities. Baptism is seen as marking the gateway to eschatological life for new converts, and it is also a powerful sign of the kind of life to which the church is called to live out in this world. That entails a commitment to 'suffering', whether physical (as slaves were to know) or economic/social, arising out of the quality of Christian obedience in a hostile world. The church is partner with old Israel in its role as a witness to the nations, and, like the servant of Isaiah (Isa. 40–55), is summoned to maintain the truth in conflict and pain. But God's presence is there, if within the shadows, and the new Israel, along with its counterpart in the OT, is to discover its role as the 'one people of God' (2. 9–10).

1 PETER – A LITERARY ANALYSIS

The plan of 1 Peter is relatively straightforward, though some attempts to find an elaborate patternistic arrangement seem more ingenious than convincing.[28] It is generally agreed that the letter divides at 2. 10 and 4. 11, thus giving a division into three parts. Those scholars who think the present letter is a pastiche made up of two documents will want to make a particularly strong break at 4. 11 with its notes of doxology and Amen. But the growing consensus wishes to maintain the unity of the letter on the grounds of a common theme throughout, the perceptions that the sequence of 'statement' followed by 'exhortation' is well known in the NT epistles, and the letter-form naturally puts eschatology at the end (4. 12–5:

---

[27] B. J. Malina, 'Christ and Time: Swiss or Mediterranean?' *CBQ* 51 (1989) 1–31.
[28] E.g. C. H. Talbert's elaborate analysis in *Perspectives on First Peter*, ch. 8.

11). Assuming, then, the letter's closely knit texture throughout, we may offer the following analysis, mainly suggested by Kendall[29] and Bénétreau.[30]

I: Christian existence (1. 3–2. 10)

After address and greeting (1. 1–2) the first major part rehearses and explains the foundation of the church's life as the people of God. The opening praise-formulation (1. 3–12) lays the groundwork for the rest of the letter, as Kendall has shown. The believers' new existence is grounded in Christ's resurrection. This is the basis for hope and points to God's guaranteed future, as God's faithfulness and human faith are conjoined in an enterprise that is paradoxically both a time of affliction and an occasion of joy.[31] The life of believers is set at 'the apex not only of salvation history but also of the cosmic drama of redemption, for even the angels are attracted by the wonder of saving grace (12)'.[32] The application is then made to live in the light of God's redeeming purpose (1. 13–2. 10) with a three-fold dimension:

(i)   in regard to the world, Christian behaviour is controlled by nonconformity and holiness (1. 13–21)

(ii) in respect of community life within the church the call is to familial love and maturity (1. 22–2. 3)

(iii) in response to God's call the church is to be a worshipping body reflecting the destiny of Christ (2. 4–10).

II: Christian living in society (2. 11–4. 11)

The life of the Christian community is placed in a contemporary setting, and the characteristic feature to be cultivated and presented is that of 'living good lives among the pagans' (2. 12, NIV). Three motivations of this ideal are displayed:

---

29 D. W. Kendall, 'The Literary and Theological Function of 1 Peter 1. 3–12' in: *Perspectives on First Peter*, ch. 6.

30 S. Bénétreau, *La première épître de Pierre*, Vaux-sur-Seine 1984, 71–3.

31 N. Brox, *Der erste Petrusbrief* EKK 21 Zurich 1979 66 calls this the central problem of the letter as defining a 'characteristic of being a Christian' in 1 Peter.

32 Kendall, 'The Literary and Theological Function', 107.

(i) God's people are called to live in a situation of conflict and suffering (2. 18–24), with slaves being particularly vulnerable to assault by harsh masters. Christ's sufferings are the model to be followed (2. 21).

(ii) The exhortation to 'do good' (2. 12) is illustrated in various ways, with special attention devoted to Christian wives and husbands (3. 1–7) as part of a code for domestic harmony and witness to the world. The concrete ways in which this encouragement to 'do good' and live exemplary lives is applied are set out (from Psalm 34) as a repudiating of vengeance, a love to one's fellows (3. 8–12) and a readiness to maintain a firm, yet conciliatory, stand for the truth (3. 13–16). The reality of evil society is the background for an elaborate credal-confessional diversion that heralds Christ's victory over all malign powers, both earthly and cosmic. In that victory (3. 22) believers have a share as they too live 'in submission to Christ the Lord' (3. 15).

(iii) As the pattern of 'suffering-leading-to-glory' begins with Christ (1. 6–7, 10–11), so it is made relevant to suffering Christians. They are called to the same vocation of suffering as their Lord (2. 21–3; 3. 9, 10–17, 18; 4. 1) and, as the eschatological hour of deliverance and vindication draws near (4. 7), they may anticipate their reward as Christ was honoured (2. 1–10). In the interim the life of the community is marked by prayer (4. 7b), practical love (4. 9) and selfless service (4. 10) – a call that evokes the praise of the readers (4. 11).

III: Christian hope for the future (4. 12–5. 11)

The third section picks up and enlarges on themes already stated in 1. 3–12 and considered in 2. 11–4. 11, with a recurrence of terms all heavily weighted with eschatological overtones (suffering, suffer, trials, little while) and imminence.

To aid the church in facing these trials the author turns to some pastoral devices: he offers a specific theodicy (4. 12–13, filling out the references in 1. 6–7); he reminds the church of the fate of its oppressors (4. 17–18), reverting to 2. 7–8, and he counsels the reiterated summons to the 'good life' (4. 19, reflecting on 2. 12).[33]

The leadership will play an important role in steadying a distressed congregation, so the example of Peter is invoked (5. 1–4) as a model of pastoral solicitude (patterned on the Good Shepherd, 2. 25).

The eschatological tensions are eased by a submissive attitude (5. 5–6) within the community as in the outside world (2: 13–17) and leads to a call to vigilance, strong faith, and hope in God's final vindication (5. 10).

Epistolary close (5. 12–14) embraces personal details and a final greeting.

TWO

THEOLOGICAL THEMES IN I PETER

God – parent and creator

Probably no document in the New Testament is so theologically oriented as I Peter, if the description is taken in the strict sense of teaching about God. The epistle is theocentric through and through, and its author has a robust faith in God which he seeks to impart to the readers. The author's mind is filled with the centrality of the divine plan and purpose in both human and cosmic affairs, from the opening exultation, 'Praise be to the God and Father of our Lord Jesus Christ' (1. 3) to the closing affirmation and appeal: 'this is the authentic grace of God; stand firm in it' (5. 12). F. W. Beare[34] pays tribute to this cardinal feature of the letter:

[The author] begins from and returns constantly to the thought of God as Creator, Father, and Judge, as the One whose will determines all that comes to pass, who shapes the destiny and determines the

---

33 W. C. van Unnik, 'The Teaching of Good Works in I Peter', *NTS* I (1954) 92–110: now in his *Sparsa Collecta. The Collected Works of W. C. van Unnik, NovT* Supplement 30: Leiden, 1980, 83–105.

34 F. W. Beare, *Commentary*, 3rd edn., 52.

actions of those whom He has chosen for His own, who sustains them through the sufferings which He sends to test them, and who at the last will vindicate them and reward them eternally.

This is a noble statement, and is amply justified.

So integral to the letter's purpose is this characterization of God that we may suppose there was a reason for its prominence. If so, we should seek to find the rationale in the readers' doubts and fears. It is clear that they were enduring much unexpected suffering (4. 12; cf. 1. 6–7; 2. 20; 3. 14) and no doubt its intensity and pain, added to its unusual character, had made the task of theodicy a necessary and urgent one. By this is meant the need for a group of Christian leaders, writing to beleaguered congregations, to explain why God permitted the trials to come and what good may be expected to flow out of them.

To offer such a theodicy 1 Peter takes care to mark out the character of God in the following ways:

(a) *God as sovereign in human affairs*. The basic reality to which Peter points is the event of God's power in raising Christ from death to life (1. 3; 3. 21) and enthroning him at his right hand (3. 22), crowned with glory (1. 21) in anticipation of his final vindication (1. 7, 13; 5. 1). On this basis the text goes on to assert – or, if not explicitly, to imply – that the trials of believers are not outside the divine will (1. 6: 'in which you rejoice, even if of necessity you are grieved for a little while at your various trials'. The phrase *ei deon*, literally 'if it is needful', 'of necessity' is not rendered in RSV nor in NRSV). On the contrary, the divine plan is said to include these sufferings so that believers' faith may be refined (1. 7) and the outcome may be ensured at the final day (1. 9). This theological concession – that if suffering comes it should not be an occasion for faith's collapse, but should be embraced as part of God's providence – is renewed at 3. 17; 4. 16.

(b) *Christ the model believer in God*. Peter uses the sufferings of Christ as a point of entry into his reassurance that God is over all events. The passion text of Isaiah 53 is used to portray the providential and the exemplary nature of what happened to Jesus in his earthly career and how he reacted to insults and injuries (2. 21–5). Those sufferings were predicted long ago (1. 10–12). The key term is in 2. 21: 'for to this [vocation of suffering] you have been called [by God], because Christ suffered for you, leaving you an example, that you should follow in his steps'. Obviously Peter is not devaluing the atoning worth of the cross (2. 24) nor advocating a mimicry of the events of the Lord's passion in Jerusalem. He seems rather to point to the spirit in which such sufferings were borne, and calls on his slave-readers (2. 18) to accept their vocation 'before God' (2. 20 *para theō*) as Jesus did. The common term is their 'calling' (2. 21) which is to live as 'servants of God' (2. 16) and to 'fear', i.e. reverence God in the whole of life, in experience of good and bad alike (2. 17).

It is through Christ that men and women come to belief in God (1. 21) and in union with Christ, as being 'in Christ' (5. 14), that true worship is made possible (2. 5) and true righteousness may be practised (2. 24). Christ is the elect one (2. 4, 7) and in him his people are chosen (1. 2) – but the privilege of being joined to Christ entails risk before the ultimate reward is gained (1. 11; 5. 6, 10).

(c) *The holy character of God.* Much is made in this letter of God's holiness as a basis for trust through Christ (3. 15: literally 'sanctify Christ as Lord') and a pattern for Christian living (1. 14–21). The Levitical text, 'You shall be holy, for I am holy' (Lev. 11. 44; 19. 2; 20. 7, 26) is cited as the foundation of the author's thought, and the link is made between the God who is holy and his people who are meant to resemble him in dedication to good and avoidance of moral evil (an abstinence ethic spelled out in practical terms in 3. 10–12).

(d) *God as Protector.* Since God is parent to believers (1. 17) who are his obedient children (1. 14) he may be trusted to watch over his own (2. 25) as a shepherd cares for sheep and a parent is responsible for the child born into a common family (1. 22–5). To harassed people caught in the throes of unexplained affliction the consoling word is given: 'Cast all your anxieties on him, for he cares for you' (5. 7).

But faith is no 'soft pillow' that exempts believers from trials, and confidence in God's overarching purpose does not preclude a time of future judgement when Christians will be assessed on the basis of their true humility (5. 5–6) and obedience. Judgment will be visited on the household of God (4. 17–19), and the stringent ethic is to remain firm in God's grace (4. 19; 5. 9, 12) while believers are preserved to the end (1. 5–9; 5. 10).

Christ, his person and achievement

1 Peter is rich in its Christological details. The name of Christ occurs twenty-two times ('Christ' is found in nine places in combination with 'Jesus', which never stands alone as it sometimes does in Paul and Hebrews). The chief emphasis is made in relation to his death and resurrection, which are two events tied together (1. 11; 3. 18) to form a unity. The main passages which elaborate this connection are 1. 3–7, 18–21; 2. 4–8, 21–5; 3. 18–22. All these sections are lyrical in style and form, and have been classified as containing fragments of early Christian creeds or hymns (see earlier). The presence of rhetorical forms such as the use of participles, couplets, and relative pronouns (notably 'who') is a tell-tale sign of liturgical speech, along with ideas drawn from parts of the OT that also figure in other NT hymnic compositions (for example, Isa. 53).

1 Peter 1. 3–7. The letter opens with a blessing (1. 3–5), following the Jewish model of the prayer language of the synagogue.[35] The focal point of praise is the act of God in raising Jesus Christ from death to new life whose quality spills over into the hope which his resurrection promises. That hope is secure in spite of sufferings that are the present lot of believers, and will come to fruition at 'the revelation of Jesus Christ' (1. 7), namely his glorious appearing at the last time (1. 5; 1. 13; 5. 1, 4). Resurrection and final advent are thus linked as providing the solid basis for what the author regards as a firm hope and secure inheritance (1. 4). The joy he inculcates is based on what he knows of Christ's presence in the present experience of believers (1. 6, 8–9).

[35] V. P. Furnish, 'Elect Sojourners in Christ: An Approach to the Theology of 1 Peter', *Perkins School of Theology Journal* 28 (1975) 1–11 (6–7).

1 Peter 1. 18–21. R. Bultmann[36] identified this little section as a Christ-hymn, and some poetic features such as the couplet in 20:

> Destined before the foundation of the world,
> But manifested at the end of the times

linked by *men . . . de* to connect the lines, are good evidence that he was correct though there is less confidence that a 'lost' introduction read, 'I believe in the Lord Jesus Christ.' Detached Christological 'tags' without the name of the person are attested in Phil. 2. 6–11; Col. 1. 15–20; 1 Tim. 3. 16, so the presence of a divine name is no necessary requirement here. In any case the name of Christ appears in the preceding verse (19). The introductory 'You know that . . .' (18) also indicates that Peter is calling upon traditional material.

The way Christ's relationship to God is pictured (20) mirrors what the author believes is true of his readers (1. 2). Both they and their Lord were 'chosen according to the fore-knowledge of God the Father'; and the Christological allusion is reinforced in 2. 6, the stone laid in Zion is 'chosen and precious' to God just as he has become 'precious' to those who are his people (2. 7). It is true that this picture language could be regarded as simply a dramatic way of highlighting God's overall supervision of both Christ's career and his people's status. Yet given all we may learn of the readers' sense of being disadvantaged in society and living at odds with their pagan neighbours (2. 11–12; 4. 3–6) it is more likely that Peter's intention is to assure those readers that both their salvation and their status are secure by being taken back into the divine counsels from the beginning. They are not at the mercy of feckless chance or historical accidents (a point explicitly made in 1. 4). It would serve Peter's purpose equally to take back the saving plan involving Christ to a similar anchorage in God's eternal purpose. Hence Christ is both the elect one and the one in whom his people are elected – a dual assertion that lies at the

---

[36] R. Bultmann, 'Bekenntnis- und Liedfragmente im ersten Petrusbrief', 1–14 (2–4) (= *Exegetica*, 286–7).

centre of Karl Barth's bid to defend and expound Calvin's doctrine for the church's comfort today.

The foreknowing choice of God is carried back to eternity and then is set in a historical framework ('at the end of the times' is 'now' for 1 Peter, as prophetic witness confirms, 1. 10–12). That historical setting is anchored in the OT – Jewish world of the Passover lamb (Exod. 12) offered in sacrifice to deliver the Israelites from bondage and permit their entry into freedom. Christ's blood shows how believers are cleansed (1. 2) in order to become God's new people.[37]

1 Peter 2. 4–8. Selwyn[38] proposed that in 2. 1–10 verses 6–8 formed a compact hymn, common to both Peter and Paul, (Rom. 9. 33) and indebted to Isaiah 8. 14 which is quoted alongside other OT texts. Windisch anticipated him in arranging the verses in lines to produce what he called 'a hymn on the holy destiny of christendom, in four strophes, 1–3, 4–5, 6–8, 9–10'.[39] But there is little support for this use of the term 'hymn' to cover a poetic passage. The main Christological interest lies in the way OT texts are pressed into service to demonstrate the 'stoneship of Christ' (as Cyprian[40] labelled these texts, based on the OT references to a (messianic) stone, as in Ps. 118. 22). As a chosen stone – Christ's appointment to this role is part of God's premundane choice – he takes on a decisive role in salvation-history. Attitudes to him, of acceptance or rejection, determine human destiny, just as the model of 'suffering/vindication', which originally pertained to the Lord (1. 11) has become extended to human beings. The church of Peter's concern was undergoing suffering; but

---

[37] W. C. van Unnik, 'The Redemption of 1 Peter 1. 18–19 and the Problem of the First Epistle of Peter', *Sparsa Collecta.* The Collected Essays of W. C. van Unnik, *NovT* Supplement 30: Leiden, 1980, 3–82.

[38] E. G. Selwyn. *Commentary,* 268–77. On the section see J. H. Elliott, *The Elect and the Holy.* An exegetical examination of 1 Peter 2. 4–10 and the phrase *basileion hierateuma NovT* Supplement 12: Leiden, 1966; E. Best, '1 Peter II. 4–10 – A Reconsideration', *NovT* 11 (1969) 270–93; K. R. Snodgrass, '1 Peter 2. 1–10: Its Formation and Literary Affinities', *NTS* 24 (1977) 97–106.

[39] H. Windisch, *Die katholischen Briefe,* 3rd edn., 58.

[40] Cyprian *Testimonies* (Treatise 12) ii.16; N. Hillyer, '"Rock-Stone" imagery in 1 Peter', *Tyndale Bulletin* 22 (1971) 58–81; C. F. D. Moule, 'Some Reflections on the "Stone *Testimonia*" in Relation to the Name Peter', *NTS* 2 (1955–6) 56–8.

eschatological vindication is on the way and it will spell doom for the faithless and the persecutors (cf. 4. 17–18; 5. 5–6).

1 Peter 2. 21–5. This letter is distinctive in the NT in the way it places side by side social teachings (slaves in 2. 18–21; wives and husbands in relationship, 3. 1–7) and Christology. To enforce the point about slaves becoming models of patient endurance under provocation, the author introduces the example of the servant of God *par excellence*, Jesus Christ. The tribute to Christ the servant is evidently based on Isaiah 53 which is explicitly cited, and the saving significance of what Christ did is drawn out in no less explicit terms (24). Yet for the author's purpose it is enough simply to indicate the suffering servant as a role model for steadfast loyalty and acceptance of wrong (21). It seems clear that at least 22–4 had an independent existence, and were taken over as a preformed unit and inserted into the exhortation. Yet both the ethical call and the soteriological teaching were part of Peter's purpose, with the link idea being the principle that, as God vindicated his servant who is now the risen Shepherd (25), so he may be trusted to take care of his people who 'walk in his steps' and commit their lives to God as Jesus did.

The sufferings of Christ have both vicarious efficacy ('He bore our sins', 24) and exemplary power ('He suffered for you, leaving you an example', 21).[41] To readers, especially those in the slave class, often victimized and without redress, the picture of Christ in these verses would be a mirror-image in which they would see their own lot and take heart from both the human experience of Jesus Christ and God's control of events in the long run.

1 Peter 3. 18–22. The fullest statement of 1 Peter's Christology lies in this difficult passage.[42] As with 2. 18–22 the immediate

---

[41] See J. H. Elliott, 'Backward and Forward "In His Steps". Following Jesus from Rome to Raymond and Beyond. The Tradition, Redaction, and Reception of 1 Peter 2. 18–25' in: F. F. Segovia (ed.), *Discipleship in the New Testament*, Philadelphia 1985, 184–209.

[42] The basic works are B. Reicke, *The Disobedient Spirits and Christian Baptism. A Study of 1 Pt. 3. 19 and its context*, Copenhagen 1946; W. J. Dalton, *Christ's Proclamation to the Spirits. A Study of 1 Peter 3. 18–4. 6*, Rome 1965, 2nd edn., 1989; M.-E. Boismard, *Quatre Hymnes Baptismales dans la première épître de Pierre* Paris, 1961.

context relates to suffering. In 3. 16–17 Christians are undergoing social ostracism and active hostility from their neighbours on account of their profession and are cautioned not to become like their adversaries. At 4. 1–6 Peter will return to this theme as his readers are counselled to 'arm yourselves also with the same intention' (4. 1, NRSV). In the interval the text is devoted to a recital of Christ's sufferings (18, NRSV) which eventually issued in his elevation to glory following the resurrection (22).

Regarding the section 3. 18–22 form-critical analysis, pioneered by Bultmann,[43] has led to a bewildering array of theories. Bultmann himself believed that a later editor glossed an original text which looked like this:

> Who suffered once for sins,
> To bring us to God
> Put to death in the flesh
> But made alive in the spirit
> in which he also preached to the imprisoned spirits;
> (but) having gone into heaven he sat at the right hand of God
> Angels and authorities and powers under his control.

Obviously a lot has been left out in this alleged 'original' version, and Bultmann is often faulted for his drastic and surgical handling of the text. Two comments may assist our understanding of Christology here. First, Bultmann is correct, we believe, in setting the couplet, 'Put to death in the flesh, but made alive in the spirit' (18) as central – a point taken up by J. T. Sanders[44] who argues that this couplet is the basis for what was later elaborated in the six-line hymn of 1 Timothy 3. 16. The latter verse gives a more complete statement on the chief element in this type of Christology: the twofold existence of Christ as incarnate-redeeming/risen-victorious. Verse 22 in our passage celebrates what the second member states tersely: he is conqueror of all cosmic spirit-powers that first-century people feared and that threatened the church as God's people. This may well be the essential point of appealing to the

---

[43] R. Bultmann, 'Bekenntnis- und Liedfragmente im ersten Petrusbrief', 1–14 (=*Exegetica*, 285–97 (287–97)).

[44] J. T. Sanders, *The New Testament Christological Hymns*, Cambridge 1971, 17–18.

Christological model in 1 Peter 3. It would bring assurance to the beleaguered Christians, when harassed and fearful, that the regnant Christ, now exalted, is Lord of all the enemies, both human and demonic, they most feared. The same ideology of suffering leading to glory and Christ's present lordship runs through other NT hymns (Phil. 2. 6–11; 1 Tim. 3. 16; Eph. 1. 22–3).[45] Access to God (3. 18) and assurance of Christ's rule over all his foes were the twin reminders most needed in the context of the letter.

The second observation is more critical of Bultmann's proposal. He has, it seems, left out a feature in the text which provides an interpretative key. By omitting the phrase 'he went' from verse 19 he has overlooked the connection with verse 22 which also has the same Greek participle, rendered 'he has gone' into heaven. Two movements are thereby involved. He went on a journey to make proclamation to the spirits in prison; he went on a subsequent journey to God's presence, thereby announcing his mastery of all spirit-powers. It cannot be accidental that these two verbs match and correspond, and they give us a much needed clue.

The passage is, in essence, a depiction of Christ's odyssey, with this journey-idea the frame. With Wengst,[46] we should trace a 'way of Christ' in progressive steps from his incarnation and death (18) to his mission to the realm of spirit-forces, followed by his exaltation and enthronement as he journeyed into heaven at the ascension. We may surmise that the spirits to which he proclaimed his message are to be equated with the spirits now subjugated. If so, the role of Christ set in the interim between death and ascension is the crucial issue on which some light is cast.

Three questions addressed to the meaning of verses 19–20

---

[45] M. Hengel, 'Hymn and Christology', *Studia Biblica* 3 (1978). Papers on Paul and Other New Testament Authors, ed. E. A. Livingstone, JSNTSS 3, Sheffield 1980, 173–97; R. P. Martin, 'New Testament Hymns: Background and Development', *ExpT* 94 (1983) 132–6.

[46] K. Wengst, *Christologische Formeln und Lieder des Urchristentums*, Gütersloh 1972, 144, 163. He designates 'six stations' on the 'way of Christ', namely, pre-existence, appearance at 'the end of time' (i.e. in the incarnation), death, resuscitation (from the dead), ascension, and the enthronement when the cosmic powers submitted.

are posed:[47] (1) Who/what are the 'spirits' Christ preached to? (2) When was the proclamation made? (3) What was its content, good or bad news? Two ancillary questions, not strictly Christological, are, what is the relation (if any) between the spirits of 3. 19 and the dead of 4. 6, since Christ evidently addressed both groups, though that is debatable? And, taking us into the meaning of 2 Peter, since W. J. Dalton's monograph[48] uses 2 Peter 2. 4–5 as the key to unlock the mysteries in 1 Peter 3. 18–22, how does the 2 Peter allusion to a judgement decree passed on fallen angels help?

Let us start with Dalton's reasoned bid to employ 2 Peter 2. 4–5 which describes the primordial account of fallen angels at work in Noah's day and their sentence of doom and gloom as a foil to praise faithful Noah and righteous Lot. This leads to the hortatory reminder in 2 Peter 2. 9 that the godly will be preserved and the evil persons, human and non-human, finally punished. This is held roughly to match the situation in 1 Peter 3 and 4. 6, and to explain why the scenario is similar. So we have a portrayal of Christ as a new Enoch (so Kelly describes him) who, in the Jewish apocalyptic literature that grew up around the Genesis story in 6. 1–8, visited the underworld and announced the fate of the wicked superbeings which were associated with Satan in his pride and downfall. In the time between his crucifixion and ascension Christ made this journey and did so for one purpose: to seal the doom of the evil powers whose regime is now, (since the enthronement in verse 22), brought to an end.

However strange-sounding this saga reads, there is no denying its evocative appeal to readers for whom notions of demon enslavement and the need to be assured of God's control of events in society around them would be real. Moreover, as a socially marginalized group (see later, pp. 124–6) their sense of powerlessness to effect change and to gain any

---

[47] In addition to Reicke and Dalton see Kelly, *Commentary*, 155–6; J. R. Michaels, *1 Peter*, WBC 49, Waco 1988, 194–222; I. H. Marshall, *1 Peter*, Leicester 1991, 124–9; W. A. Grudem, *1 Peter*, Leicester 1988, 157–9 but with an idiosyncratic view of 'spirits in prison' as being 'in prison' in Peter's day. This proposal is refuted by Marshall, *1 Peter*, 125–7.

[48] W. J. Dalton, *Christ's Proclamation to the Spirits*, 2nd edn., 1989.

place of dignity and freedom would be just as real. Hence, the picture of a Christ who entered evil's domain to rob it of its power and to emerge victorious would have immediate relevance. This dramatic Christology (later to be described as Christus Victor, but implying a suffering Christ on the road to his glory, 1. 11) is a master theme in 1 Peter, and well suited to the first readers' situation and contingencies. Moreover, this presentation, if G. Aulén's historical and theological study[49] is appreciated, has not lost its appeal to some sections of modern society. In spite of our technological sophistication and scientific attitude – for which 'spirits in prison' and journeys to heaven are alien, almost nonsense categories of expression – the modern person still needs to share the confidence that 1 Peter is designed to inculcate that our lives are not at the mercy of ruthless forces outside their control, and that the beneficent power called God has entered our human experience of suffering and distress – and triumphed.

The one feature of this scenario (in 3. 18–22) on which later creed-makers and medieval dramatists, artists, sculptors, and preachers fastened was the 'descent into hell' and (as a consequence) the 'spoiling' of the world of the dead. The phrase 'He descended into hell' is found as part of a creed adopted in May 359 CE at Sirmium and then recited according to the legend in Rufinus that each apostle made his personal contribution to the formula. Thomas said – so the sermons of pseudo-Augustine tell us – he 'descended into hell' as he added this line to the creed. There is an anticipation of the teaching in Ignatius, *Trallians* 9 which contains a confession-like formulation: Jesus 'was truly crucified and died in the sight of beings in heaven, on earth and under the earth' (a wide scope drawn from the NT hymn Phil. 2. 6–11). Yet it is the so-called Dated Creed of Sirmium in which the teaching is first firmly attested.

Others parts of the New Testament have contributed to the idea that Christ's death affected the realm of the dead as he 'went down' to that region (a *descensus ad inferos*), especially Matthew 12. 39–40; Acts 2. 27, 31; Romans 10. 6–8; Ephe-

---

[49] G. Aulén, *Christus Victor* London, 1931.

sians 4. 8–10; and Revelation 5. 13.[50] Selwyn (*Commentary*, p. 322) regards it as 'part of the current coin of New Testament teaching', appealing of course to 1 Peter 3. 19; 4. 6 though we should note that the Petrine texts say nothing about Christ's going *down* to the underworld; rather the direction of his mission (we have argued) is upward, to the heavenly realm.

There is some debate as to the evolution of this line of the creed and the earliest attested form (at Sirmium[51]) contains the elaboration: he 'descended to hell, and regulated things there, whom the gatekeepers of hell saw and shuddered' (cf. Jas. 2. 19). The shorter version without the elaboration is the one that survives in the traditional Apostles' Creed as it is used today in liturgical worship. It is interesting the way Christ's descent to the underworld grew from the simple observation in Augustine that 1 Peter 3. 19 meant a mission of Christ to the contemporaries of Noah's day prior to his incarnation to a full-blown dramatization of the 'harrowing of hell'.[52] That is, the developed scenario moves from an assurance that there is resurrection-hope for pre-Christian saints (in Noah's time) to Christ's mysterious activity during the 'three days of death' (Good Friday to Easter), as it came to be known. In that time period he defeated the demons in the lower regions, spoiled the realm of the dead (hinted at in Rev. 1. 18), and liberated humankind from its bondage to an evil empire. Caesarius of Arles, in his sermons, makes Christ like a lion which destroys the dragon (Satan) not on the cross (where Col. 2. 15 fixes the dramatic encounter) but in the underworld, 'he descended to hell in order to rescue us from the jaws of the cruel dragon'. We may compare the dramatic interlude in the *Gospel of Peter* 41–2 and the even more dramatic encounter in the underworld based on Psalm 24 in *The Acts of Pilate* 21–4.

Two other developments are part of this piece of Christian imaginative reflection on the salvific work of Christ. What may

[50] C. E. B. Cranfield, 'The Interpretation of 1 Peter iii.19 and iv.6', *ExpT* 69 (1958) 369–72.

[51] J. N. D. Kelly, *Early Christian Creeds*, 2nd edn., London 1960, 289–90, 378–83.

[52] See J. A. MacCulloch, *The Harrowing of Hell*, Edinburgh, 1930. See for some more discussion, R. P. Martin, *Carmen Christi*, Cambridge/Grand Rapids 1967, 1983, 217–19.

have begun in Tertullian as a way to emphasize the completeness of the Lord's identification with our human lot in suffering and desolation (in line with 1 Peter's teaching, we believe) was expanded to hold out the hope of universal salvation. It is difficult to deny in this drama a protest (voiced in Ignatius) against Docetism, that is, against the supposition that Christ's earthly life was phantom and unreal. We know Ignatius' opponents took this view and that he uses the creed to refute them. Yet, the more the completeness of Christ's link with the human race is stressed, the more weight is given to the hope that all people are included in the scope of his salvation. The pastoral element is often taken up from this conclusion (in such as F. D. Maurice) with the expectation that those who have died without having heard or responded to the gospel are not unblessed, since Christ's post-mortem mission was (it is said) directed to these, whether as people who lived before Christ's coming (3. 19) or the unevangelized deceased (4. 6). Exegetical considerations make it unlikely that either meaning for Peter's readers can be sustained, since the mission of 3. 19 is more probably one of sealing the doom of the demons and 4. 6 seems to speak of Christian dead who, though they are now deceased, had the good news presented to them in their lifetime.

The other tangential development has to do with the theology of Atonement. For Calvin (with an influence on Karl Barth) the journey to Hades (the underworld understood as Gehenna, the place of punishment) is to be regarded in literal fashion. Calvin argued that Christ's death involved his sin-bearing activity to the fullest extent and that he was consigned to hell as the utmost limit of penal endurance (he bore 'the terrible torments of a condemned and forsaken man', *Institutes* 2. 16. 10–11). The cry of Mark 15. 34 is often associated with this terrifying prospect of forsakenness. Yet Peter stops short of this conclusion, however much he sees Christ's sufferings as vicarious and sin-atoning (2. 24; 3. 18). The part of Calvin's theorizing that may still claim validity is the assurance that no part of human experience, however bitter and alienated from God, is outside the range of God's interest and Christ's power to touch. The link with Hebrews, with its picture of a sympathetic and suffering saviour, is strong at this point (Heb. 2. 14–8; 4. 15–6; 9. 28; 12. 2).

The distinctive elements in 1 Peter's picture of Christ are summed up in the title, 'Lord' (3. 15). His phases of existence cover the range of (a) his life-in-God before his coming to earth (1. 20; 2. 6; cf. 1. 11 where the 'Spirit of Christ' was active in the OT prophets); (b) his incarnate and human life marked by suffering (1. 11; 2. 21–4; 3. 18, NRSV; 4. 1–13; 5. 1) and death (3. 18), and his resurrection (1.3; 3. 18) which vindicated his obedience; and (c) his final glory (1. 7, 13; 4. 13; 5. 1). No attempt is made to work out the precise relationship of the Son to the Father, and 'Son of God' is not found as a title. 'Servant of God' is implied in the indebtedness to Isaiah 53 (in 2. 22–4), a Christological label that quickly fell into disuse in the later apostolic era and beyond.

There is no denying the immediate appeal of this Christology, which relates Christ intimately to the individual believers (1. 8–9) as well as the church's destiny as the elect people of God (2. 1–10). Christ's present status is one of exaltation (2. 7; 3. 22), yet that dignity does not rob him of an intimacy with his followers who find their life 'in Christ' (5. 14), i.e. in union with him as their lover and protector (1. 8; 2. 25).

The Holy Spirit

The Spirit, sometimes surnamed 'Holy' (1. 12) but referred to also simply as the Spirit (1. 2; 4. 14) or 'Spirit of Christ' (1. 11), does not figure prominently in this letter. Yet it will not do to conclude (as Beare does[53]) that 'the Spirit has fallen into eclipse ... in First Peter' and so infer that the document reflects conditions in a period of spiritual stagnation and ecclesiological rigidity and formalism.

The mention of the role of the Spirit in sanctifying the church is very much in the Pauline tradition (1 Cor. 3. 16–17; 6. 19; 1 Thess 4. 7–8; 2 Thess 2. 13; the exact terminology is

---

[53] F. W. Beare, *Commentary*, 3rd edn., 55.

the same in the last reference given). The work of the Spirit in inspiring prophets (1. 10–12) has its parallel in Paul according to one interpretation that sees NT prophets alluded to here (so Selwyn who argues that the prophetic witness is illustrated in such leaders as Agabus in Acts 11. 28 and in the charismatic figures referred to in 1 Cor. 14. 3 and following). But the function of the prophets in 1 Peter hardly tallies with these depictions. It is more natural to see the allusion as relating to OT prophetic witness to the coming messiah. The chief reason for this identification is that Peter puts some distance in time between the prophets mentioned and his readers (1. 12) and so does not regard them as contemporaries. 'The Spirit of Christ' is thus a description of their function. They were Israel's prophetic leaders who divined by inspiration that God's kingdom would bring with it an anointed figure (messiah) whose ultimate glory would come only along a road of suffering and sorrow. In Christian terms this is the prophecy of a suffering messiah, read in Isaiah 53 (as in Acts 8. 30–5; 1 Pet. 2. 22–4). It is on the basis of this Christological witness in the OT that Christian missionaries, aided by the same Holy Spirit, have brought the good news to the Asian communities that Peter addressed (12). The function of the Spirit is at once revelatory and dynamic, and is not quite the same as the mode of inspiration and interpretation of scripture, outlined in 2 Peter 1. 19–21 at a later stage of development.

The Spirit's ministry at 4. 14 has a practical and pastoral character. Persecuted believers are comforted in their trials by the assurance that the divine Spirit like Yahweh's Shekinah or glorious covering (a rabbinic term for the divine presence based on Exod. 24. 15–18) rests as a protecting shield over them. The strengthening of the Spirit in time of stress is in line with what is promised in Matthew 10. 19–20; Mark 13. 11; Luke 12. 11–12. The manifestation of divine glory in the case of Stephen (called a 'witness' in Acts 22. 20) is referred to in Acts 7. 55 and makes the same connection, with a different scenario, though the term *martys* ('witness') is given in 5. 1. Perhaps this connection is made in acknowledgment of Peter's martyrdom in Rome in 65 CE. The common element is the power the Spirit gives to maintain a faithful witness, especially under trial.

In sum, the role of the Holy Spirit as briefly touched on in this letter is perhaps more pervasive than the few references would suggest. Most of the main elements of the work of the Spirit in relation to the believer and the church mentioned elsewhere in the NT, especially in Paul, are here on display, if not developed at length. His task is that of making the chosen people a choice people by promoting holy living (1. 2), a function that led Peter to include an extended treatment of 'holiness' (1. 14–22; cf. 3. 15) which, in typically Pauline fashion, carries the twofold side of separation from moral evil and devotion to good (see 3. 13). The levitical holiness code (Lev. chs. 17–26) is the ground-plan of Peter's thought, but the cultic and ceremonial ideas are replaced by a process of 'de-sacralizing' or 'spiritualization' (2. 5: 'spiritual sacrifices'; cf. Heb. 13. 15), while losing none of the serious intent and practical application, as befits worship of the holy one of Israel (1. 16).

The Spirit too has a ministry that may be classified under the term 'eschatological'. This means that Peter's readers were encouraged to think of themselves as living in the new age of God's salvation, heralded by the ancient prophets (1. 10–11) and brought to realization by the coming of Israel's messiah (1. 11–12). So the Spirit is 'messianic', meaning a guarantee of the new era already begun and soon to be finalized (4. 14: 'Spirit of glory' is linked with the 'glories' to come, in 1. 11; 5. 1). The pivot on which the past salvation and future hope turn is the present reality of the Spirit's power in the community, now that Jesus is already 'glorified' (1. 21; 3. 22) in anticipation of his future coronation (5. 1, 4), which will entail his people's honour as well.

All this is commonly accepted and experienced NT teaching about the vitality of Christian life and charismatic fervour – a fact that puts 1 Peter in the main flow of early Christianity, yet with a distinctive idiom and emphasis. The latter is no doubt explained by the letter's purpose to encourage believers in time of acute distress and inexplicable trials. This setting may equally account for the inbuilt tension between the call to individual and corporate responsibility (explicit in 3. 8–9; 4. 10–11) and the (implicit) summons to respect the leadership of the church whose special problems are brought to the surface in 5. 1–5. Peter evidently saw no incompatibility between communities where every Christian had an individual role to play (akin to the assumptions in 1 Cor. 12) and communities which had honoured oversight (no less prominent in 1 Cor. 16. 17–18 where leading Corinthian figures are commended for all to respect and follow).

The Christian community: its problems and responses

The nature of the Christian life in 1 Peter is set forth in distinctive ways. But it is essential, as a background to this discussion, to have in mind two questions to do with the historical circumstances in which the letter was written and sent to Christian communities in Asia. One issue concerns the kinds of 'persecution' in view, one kind, real and present, the other kind about to, or likely to, happen in the near future. The second matter has to do with the letter's unity. We consider these two questions in order.

(1) Modern study – with a few exceptions (for example, Beare, Reicke[54]) – has reached a conclusion that the references to suffering in this epistle have much more to do with local outbursts of opposition than with an official state policy of punishing Christians as such, that is, on profession of their faith as subversive. It is true that such hostility was keenly felt by the readers and so needed to be addressed by the writer. Kelly, therefore, writes of the author's purpose that it is seen as one 'of the sustaining and encouraging Asian Christians' whose 'troubles are the ever-felt background of every paragraph' he writes.[55]

F. W. Beare accepts the role of suffering as a characteristic of

---

[54] F. W. Beare, *Commentary*, 3rd edn., 29–34, 188; B. Reicke, *The Epistles of James, Peter and Jude*, AB 37, Garden City 1964, xv–xxix; cf. J. Knox, 'Pliny and 1 Peter', *JBL* 72 (1953) 187–89.

[55] Kelly, *Commentary*, 25.

Peter's audience. He proceeds to argue that the section
4. 12–16 can mean only that Christians were being accused of
a political charge and were suffering 'on account of the name'
of Christ as sedition-mongers and enemies of the Roman state.
B. Reicke has a parallel view of 1 Peter as issuing restraints
against a Christian zealot or nationalistic movement involved
in seeking to overthrow the Roman government. But both
Beare and Reicke have been effectively answered by C. F.
Sleeper who denies that the Christians in 1 Peter's sights were
so politically motivated.[56] 1 Peter hardly pictures the churches
as forming a political group, subversive of the state, and as was
indicated earlier there are several counter-arguments that tell
against this setting of the epistle at the time in the early second
century, according to Pliny when the mere profession and
practice of Christianity was regarded as punishable by death.

(a) Nothing in the letter indicates an official action against
the churches. After reviewing the data in the letter itself, Kelly
concludes that because 'there is no evidence of any very extensive persecution initiated by the government in the 1st or early
2nd centuries', there is no reason to quarrel with 'the impression which the letter as a whole conveys [which] is not of
juridical prosecutions by the government ... but of an atmosphere of suspicion, hostility and brutality on the part of the
local population which may easily land Christians in trouble
with the police'.[57]

(b) 1 Peter has no explicit allusion to official inquisition or
torture, such as was practised in Pontus-Bithynia in Pliny's
time (112 CE, Pliny, *Epp*. 10. 96f.). The descriptions of the trials
the readers were enduring (1. 6) and the ill-treatment meted
out to them (3. 13–4. 11), along with the 'fiery ordeal'
(4. 12–19), suggest that the hardships were more personal and
confined to one area, 'originating in the hostility of the surrounding population', as Kelly observes.[58]

(c) On the other hand, sufferings of Christians are part of the
general attitude taken to them in other places outside the

[56] C. F. Sleeper, 'Political Responsibility according to 1 Peter', *NovT* 10 (1968)
270–86.
[57] Kelly, *Commentary*, 29.   [58] Kelly, *Commentary*, 10.

Anatolian provinces, if we take seriously the remark in 5. 9, 'knowing that the same experience of suffering is required of your brotherhood throughout the world' (RSV). This reference is regarded by Kelly as crucial in fixing the kind of hostility undergone by the church at the time of 1 Peter's writing. The troubles are, then, in no way exceptional, but have their counterpart in other places. Local outbursts of mob violence may well account for these pinpricks which no doubt were very real and painful if localized (suggested by 4. 1–4).

Though we may not be able, with any degree of precision, to pin-point these trials and place their outbreak in any specific historical or social time-frame, they do form a background for Peter's tract of encouragement and hope, as stated in 5. 12. The presence and pressure of trials explain the strong eschatological perspective in which the author places the experience of his readers; and equally the threats and evils that bear upon the readers make it all the more pertinent that their behaviour and reaction should be exemplary.

(2) So far we have assumed that the entire letter called 1 Peter addresses a single problem in connection with the churches' suffering. But this is not a fully accepted idea. C. F. D. Moule[59] has raised the possibility that, as there looks to be a distinct break at 4. 11 which records a doxology and an Amen at an apparent close of a letter, we should think of our 1 Peter as made up of two separate compositions, 1. 3–4. 11 and 4. 12–5. 14. He furthermore suggests that there is a change in which the afflictions are viewed in the two parts. In 2. 11–4. 11 the sufferings are in prospect, but in 4. 12–5. 11 they are actually happening to the readers. In this way he accounts for the change in the tenses of the verbs and explains what he detects as a shift in the tone and atmosphere of the two sections in the letter. In the first, the style is more calm and measured, betraying a placid mood, whereas at 4. 12 (he says, in company with Beare) the letter begins to evince a more fearful and nervous atmosphere. The style is more direct and simple. For Beare the second part from 4. 12 to the end has 'no

[59] C. F. D. Moule, 'The Nature and Purpose of 1 Peter', *NTS* 3 (1956–7) 1–11.

carefully constructed periods or nicely balanced rhythms and antitheses ... it has the quick and nervous language of a letter written in haste and under tension'.[60]

Kelly has criticized this line of reasoning on linguistic and contextual grounds.[61] He maintains that there is no clear and consistent distinction made in the tenses of the verbs and that the entire letter is shot through with the motif of 'persecution' – or at least of believers' trials which are then traced to the hostile treatment to be expected of minority groups living in a pagan environment. This element pervades the letter and gives it the character of a persecution tract, offering encouragement and guidance to Christians in a socially determined slave-group who were undergoing the threat of serious reprisals on account of their faith. To this statement of social standing of the readers which made them vulnerable to opposition (elaborated by such studies as J. H. Elliott and L. Goppelt, with D. L. Balch[62] seeking to relate their condition within Roman households where women were exposed to pressures to conform to state religion and patriarchal norms and to show such conformity in obedience, order and harmony) one other point may be added. There is evidence from within the letter itself (for example, 1. 22–3; 2. 2–3; 3. 21) that the readers were newly won converts, and on that account persecution and deprivation of their civil rights in a now alien environment would be all the harder to understand and to bear.

These two matters outlined above set the stage for some consideration of the style of community living Peter anticipates his readers will want to follow, in the circumstances of their lot as minority groups in a difficult social milieu.

(a) For 1 Peter the Christian life is *centred in hope* (1. 3; 1. 21; 3. 5; 3. 15) and sustained by a faith in God whose purposes are known in Christ (1. 21; 4. 11). God is acknowledged in the opening prayer-thanksgiving (1. 3) as the one who raised Jesus

---

[60] Beare, *Commentary*, 3rd edn., 26.   [61] Kelly, *Commentary*, 183–4.

[62] See the latest phase of the discussion in J. H. Elliott and D. L. Balch. Their two essays are in C. H. Talbert (ed.), *Perspectives on First Peter*, Macon, GA, 1986, chs. 4 and 5, with critique and review of both writers in P. J. Achtemeier, 'Newborn Babes' etc. *To Touch the Text*, 216–22.

from the dead and exalted him to the heights of honour (1. 21; 3. 21–2). This is Peter's starting-point and the cardinal principle of his theology, both doctrinal and practical.

It is not surprising, therefore, that this letter has been called an epistle of hope. L. Goppelt[63] comments that 1 Peter orients the Christian's existence primarily to hope, where Paul's chief focus is on faith, yet there is no bid to play off the one Christian quality against the other, as verses such as 1. 5, 8, 21; 4. 19; 5. 9 highlight the active role faith is said to have in the securing of initial salvation and in its further maintenance.

(b) *Obedience* to the call of the good news, voiced by preachers who came to the Asian provinces (1. 12; 4. 6?), was the response the readers have made (1. 22, 23). The description given in 1. 14 is that they have become 'children of obedience' which includes both their initial response to the one who called them out of their dark pagan past into the new light of the Christian hope (2. 9) as God's people (2. 10) and the characteristic of the way of life now begun. Like Sarah, Christian women are to render obedience to their unbelieving spouses in the hope that those who do not yet 'obey' (God) will be won over (3. 1–6). Failure to heed the gospel call will carry dire consequences (4. 17); yet the outlook of 1 Peter is consistently optimistic, and he in turn is 'hopeful' that his readers will see good results in their witness.

Witness to the world marks out the Christian's obedience, whether to God or the structures of contemporary society (for example, 2. 13–17). As part of a life committed to God's way (2. 20; 4. 19) the author encourages the exercise of self-control (1. 13; 2. 11, 16; 4. 7) and, for members of the slave-class who were subject to harassment, the need is to be restrained and not retaliatory (see 2. 18–25). Especially when the slaves are guilty of no offence and have masters who are harsh (2. 18–20) and vindictive, the temptation to be sullen and spiteful would be natural. Peter calls on the readers to act in a different way, and appeals to the highest of examples. That example is in the suffering Lord whose attitude to his detractors was mirrored in

---

[63] L. Goppelt, *Der erste Petrusbrief*, 95.

Isaiah 53. 'He did not revile' those who insulted him becomes a text as a model to set the standard, and the same admonition is picked up in the general advice of 3. 9, with its appeal now to the 'righteous person' of Psalm 34 who turns aside from vengeance and anger even when provoked by evil people (3. 12). A similar situation to the slaves is implied in 3. 14, with a Christological model in 3. 18.

The positive side to this call to a better outlook under trial is that others will be impressed and influenced. 'Holiness' is therefore a part of the church's face as shown to the world, in order to present a picture of attractive living (1. 16–18) and to reflect the character of God whose children the readers are said to be by birth into his family (1. 22–5; 2. 1–2). Peter's use of Leviticus chs. 17–26 (the so-called 'Holiness Code' of the priestly source of the Pentateuch) enforces his point which is elaborated in 2. 4–10. There the church's role as the holy people of the new Israel, in succession to historical Israel, is brought out in such a way as to emphasize the practical issue: you were called to be God's own people, set apart for his service by the Holy Spirit's activity (1. 2) in order to carry his holy name to the nations (2. 9).[64]

Holy living is spelled out in the intensely practical and down-to-earth terms. Christians are summoned to be courteous and kind (3. 8) within their fellowship and outside in the world (3. 15). The epitome is given in the need to keep one's conscience clear and to practise 'good behaviour' (3. 16), thereby making the Christian way an appealing and attractive option. Ethical values are to be displayed, but also internalized by the cultivating of the 'gentle and tranquil spirit' (3. 4). This is much more highly prized than outward and ostentatious show (3. 3). Christian women are invited to pay attention to these qualities, with a missionary purpose always in view (3. 1–2) even when the marital situation looks hopeless (3. 6; they were fearful of being terrorized).

(c) On a broader front the Christians' attitude to *the ruling*

---

[64] This is emphasized by Achtemeier, 'Newborn Babes' etc. in a way that counterbalances recent sociological exegesis. See earlier, p. 100.

authorities in the state and the home is a major topic in our letter. The theme is a leading one in the 'household code' of 2. 13–3. 8. We may note the following points, well illustrated by Carolyn Osiek[65] in her study of the social setting of the New Testament. First, the teaching in a stylized form characteristic of set 'rules of behaviour' is introduced by the exhortation to everyone to be submissive to all legitimate political and domestic authority as to God (2. 13–17). Much debate has surrounded the term 'submission', and feminist theology has rightly questioned the validity of the teaching as understood by this emotive word, so it is well to propose a definition. As seen by 1 Peter it is not anything demeaning or debasing; it is not cringing abject fear before another person; it is not blind obedience born out of terror (3. 6). Rather it is the rational response of a person or group to higher authority within the cultural context of the day, and controlled by motives of respect, honour, and concern for the well-being of an orderly society or household.

Second, references to parents and children in 1 Peter's setting are lacking, and the order husbands–wives found in other NT documents is reversed. Third, there is no exhortation to masters, and the section devoted to slaves is expanded into a commentary on the suffering of Christ based on Isaiah 53. Fourth, the exhortation to the wives encourages obedience to the husbands (3. 6) after the example of Sarah's attitude of Abraham, in the light of Genesis 18. 12. Finally, the beginning of the exhortation to the wives (3. 1) betrays signs of a situation of domestic conflict and its resolution: the virtuous submission of the wives to their pagan husbands may lead to the latter's conversion.

D. L. Balch has proposed that the final point gives the clue to the meaning of the code in 1 Peter. It functions as a defensive apologetic in answer to the slanderous accusation of misconduct on the part of newly won Christian women. In response 1 Peter calls for order and decorous behaviour in the

---

65 C. Osiek, *What are they saying about the Social Setting of the New Testament?* New York 1984, 73–83. See too D. L. Balch, 'Hellenization/Acculturation in 1 Peter', in *Perspectives on First Peter*, ch. 5.

light of such (hypothetical) rumours of social disturbance and anarchy. This leads Balch to maintain that 1 Peter's social manifesto stresses assimilation and acculturation within the framework of Roman society where household management techniques were based on the acceptance of good order and equilibrium.

Balch's theory has been faulted by Elliott[66] and Osiek on the score that 1 Peter's frame of reference is more the divine household of the church as a holy society than a sociological paradigm drawn from contemporary ideals. There is less of social conformity and adaptation to the surrounding ethos in 1 Peter; rather the chief referent and controlling metaphor in 1 Peter's role for the church as the Christian community are seen in the picture of the new people of God who are called to be both a holy nation in an alien world and a missionary force like the servant figure in Deutero-Isaiah (so Achtemeier[67]), as we noted earlier (p. 94). The merit of seeing social instructions in the light of OT testimonies and prefigurements is not to deny the cultural setting of 1 Peter, but to view the destiny of the churches in 1 Peter as in direct succession to the OT models and metaphors cast for the people of God.

(d) A group that comes in for special notice is *the leaders in the Christian communities* (5. 1–5).[68] These people are divided into two sub-groups, the elders and the younger ones. Eldership evidently is Peter's term to denote a class of churchly officers to whom the case and protection of God's church, called his flock (as in 2. 25), are entrusted. The divine shepherd is the ultimate authority (5. 4) and he will reward faithful service at his glorious appearing. The human shepherds are accorded some authority (5. 2), with the pattern drawn from Israel's leaders in Ezekiel 34.[69] Yet, like Israel's 'shepherds' (Ezek. 34. 2–6),

---

[66] J. H. Elliott, in *Perspectives on First Peter*, ch. 4. See too Antoinette Wire's review article on Elliott and Balch in *Religious Studies Review* 10 (1984) 209–16.

[67] P. J. Achtemeier, 'Newborn Babes' etc., 235–6 and Sharon Clark Pearson's unpublished dissertation.

[68] J. H. Elliott, 'Ministry and Church Order in the NT: A Traditio-Historical Analysis (1 Pt 5:1–5 and par.)', *CBQ* 32 (1970) 367–91.

[69] Ezekiel chs. 8–11 may well have paved the way for this indebtedness to Ezekiel 34 if W. L. Schutter's argument (*Hermeneutic and Composition in 1 Peter*, 153–66) is cogent.

these leaders are guilty of negligence and an overbearing attitude that reflects their avarice and desire to domineer (compare 3 John). Peter's rebuke is targeted at such leadership, charging that such failure is a betrayal of the ministerial calling. The role model of the leader lies in humble service whether the objects of that service are the congregation (5. 3) or the mutual interests of all concerned (5. 5). All the members are involved in this responsibility for the whole group (4. 10–11).

The 'younger' (5. 5) as a term for others in the community evidently denotes a junior branch of ecclesiastical oversight; and, as they are specifically enjoined to be in submission to the (ruling) elders, it suggests that they were proving restive and rebellious. Peter's charge to them is to hold their station and not to go beyond the limits. It is set in an argument that runs parallel with his call to slaves (2. 18) and wives (3. 1–6), as well as in the more general call to submission to the ruling powers (2. 13–14).

The overarching rubric under which 'Peter', as a fellow-elder and authoritative witness (5. 1), grapples with some severe pastoral problems in those Asian communities is the place of 'humility' in Christian living. So the narrow appeal in 5. 5 is broadened at 5. 6 (returning to the theme already touched on in 3. 8, 'to be humble-minded') to include all the members within its scope. All are reminded of the general dictum given out in 5. 5, drawn from Proverbs 3. 34: 'God opposes the proud, but gives grace to the humble'. This sentiment is characteristic of the wisdom teaching in early Judaism (for example, Sirach 2. 1–18) as well as in the hortatory sections of the Wisdom literature of Hebrew scripture; it is exemplified too in Jesus' teaching (Luke 14. 11; 18. 14; Matt. 23. 12) as well as in early Jewish Christianity (Luke 1. 52; Jas. 1. 9; 4. 10).

Singular here is the pastoral call to trust (5. 7) in the face of imminent mortal danger (5. 8–9) and the pressure to succumb to present trials (5. 9–10). Peter's intention to hold up humility as a needed virtue is complemented by his hortatory reminder that the end will soon come ('when you have suffered for a little

while', 5. 10; cf. 1. 6; 4. 7 and maybe 3. 17[70]) and will bring
with it the believers' vindication and promotion to honour
(5. 6). This hope naturally leads on to what may be regarded
as 1 Peter's most impressive and characteristic moral quality,
'endurance'.

(e) The clarion call *to remain steadfast and firm* in the face of
life's problems and the opposition's hostility sounds in various
ways throughout this letter (1. 13, 21; 4. 19; 5. 9–11) even if
the imperative is heard only once: 'stand firm' in God's grace
(5. 12). In apocalyptic literature, both Jewish and Christian,
such an exhortation to remain steadfast in the teeth of life's
trials is matched by a reminder of God's sovereign control of
events and his pledge to bring his faithful people through to
ultimate reward. This expectation is in the background of our
letter (1. 7; 4. 13; 5. 4, 10–11). In the interim the beleaguered
churches can only wait in hope, upheld by divine grace,
fortified by prayer (3. 7; 4. 7), and expectant that before long
their trials will be over. They should in the meanwhile do
nothing to provoke opposition as they maintain a good character with a clear conscience (2. 12; 3. 16–17) and honour
their baptismal pledge[71] (3. 21) to be loyal to Christ their Lord
(3. 15).

True, they cannot avoid giving the impression of being a
people 'set apart' (holy means this, in one of its several shades
of meaning) and socially distinct (2. 11–12; 4. 4) in the ways
discussed earlier (p. 125). They will be summoned to give a
rationale for their faith (3. 15); and they should be ready with
a reasoned statement, provided they are prepared to do it with
'gentleness and reverence', not evincing a stubbornness and
'inflexible obstinacy' that so irritated Roman governors at a
later time (Pliny, *Epp.* 10. 96, 3) and emperors like Marcus
Aurelius (*Med.* 11.3) for whom Christian 'boldness' was taken
to be no better than 'sheer cussedness' (Gr. *psilē parataxis*). That

---

[70] If J. R. Michaels' translation is accepted: 'It is better to suffer now for doing right
than to suffer later (at the judgment) for doing wrong (by betraying the faith)',
'Eschatology in 1 Peter', *NTS* 13 (1966–7) 394–401.
[71] R. E. Nixon, 'The Meaning of "Baptism" in 1 Peter 3. 21', *Studia Evangelica* 4
(Oxford, 1968) 437–441.

would be the less attractive face of endurance, which 1 Peter evidently warns against.

In summary, the social setting of churches, which were facing a bitter experience of opposition felt by those whose social station made them vulnerable since they were politically impotent, dictated a type of Christian living appropriate to the occasion. There is no bid to overthrow the social order or foment a slave uprising. There is no call to disobedience, whether civil or activist. The ethical admonitions operate within the limit of 'what is possible': honour to those in power, both good and evil-minded (2. 17; 3. 17) and a caution to stay within the contemporary social structures as submissive and peace-making. 'Live as servants of God' (2. 16) applies to all the sub-groups in the Asian churches, and clear warnings are registered to steer clear of political entanglements (4. 15) which, in that day and circumstance, could only end in disaster and snuff out the church's very existence. The 'interim ethic' that lives in the present in hope of a divine vindication in the coming age is very much what 1 Peter's eschatological encouragement to 'endure until the end' is all about.

CHRISTIANITY ACCORDING TO 1 PETER[72]

It is a fairly obvious deduction, from the ground we have surveyed, that much in 1 Peter is distinctive and expressed in an unusual idiom that belongs to this writing. Sometimes the tell-tale signs are seemingly small: Peter likes the verb 'to suffer' used of Christ's death, where Paul and other NT writers prefer the more simple, 'He died' (1 Cor. 15. 3; Rom. 6. 5–11; Heb. 9. 15, 22; but see Heb. 9. 26). We may trace this unusual feature to the way Peter uses the sufferings of Christ as a point of reference to connect with his readers' sufferings as Christ's followers. The picture of Jesus as an example (2. 21) belongs also to the same pastoral-paraenetic concern. Paul only rarely (if at all) makes the earthly character and patient endurance of Jesus the ground for his ethical appeal (Rom. 15. 1–3; and Phil.

---

[72] See W. C. van Unnik's article with this title, *ExpT* 68 (1956–7) 79–83.

2. 5–11 which is more disputable). Peter shares with Hebrews a more direct approach by holding up before his readers the presentation of Jesus as faith's exemplar and living embodiment (Heb. 12. 1–3). But in this regard 1 Peter stands apart, since the use of Isaiah 53 as a role model for human suffering, developed in 2. 18–25,[73] is not the customary way the prophetic passage is employed in the early understandings of the death of Christ, seen in the soteriological tags in Romans 4. 25; 8. 34.

One more illustration of the distinctiveness of 1 Peter may be mentioned. His emphasis on hope runs through the letter and gives it a deep structural unity (1. 3, 13, 21; 3. 5, 15, 20). Once more the historical and situational contingencies of writing to a group of congregations under fire and threatened by loss of nerve may well explain Peter's desire to infuse new life-through-hope into jaded spirits. The closest parallel would be in the letter to the Hebrews where hope also plays a key role (Heb. 6. 19–20; 11. 1) and addresses a parallel situation. Its readers too were enduring suffering and were victims of loss of confidence – but for different reasons (Heb. 10. 32–5). In their case the conflicts were more domestic and internal and there was a theological questioning about the coming of Christ in glory (Heb. 10. 37–9). In 1 Peter the hostility is directed at the church from outside, and there seems to be no uncertainty about their final salvation, even if the author does tie the basis of hope to the imminent appearing of the Lord (1 Pet. 1. 5, 13; 4. 7).

It should not be concluded that 1 Peter is different from other comparable NT books in every respect, though there is much in the letter that gives it a distinctive flavour and makes it less likely to be a pale reflection of Paul and his school.[74] It

---

73 J. W. Thompson, ' "Be Submissive to your Masters" – A Study of 1 Peter 2. 18–25', *Restoration Quarterly* 9 (1966) 66–78 (74–8); for a treatment that denies the use of any source except Isa. 53 see T. P. Osborne, 'Guide Lines for Christian Suffering: A Source-Critical and Theological Study of 1 Peter 2, 21–5', *Bib* 64 (1983) 381–408.

74 Elliott's seminal discussion and conclusion in 'The Rehabilitation of an Exegetical Step-Child', *JBL* 95 (1976) 243–54, reprinted in *Perspectives on 1 Peter*, ch. 1, remain valid when he speaks of a 'liberation of 1 Peter from its "Pauline bondage" ' and

obviously shares much in terms of the main Christian affir-
mations, and expresses these in noble language, often drawn
from what appear to be early credal materials: God is the
parent and protector of his people; Christ is the divine revelation, once put to death for human sins and now elevated to the
rank of Lord of all cosmic powers as well as the church; the
Spirit as the agent of revelation and mission; and the people of
God, with roots and anchorage in ancient Israel, called to be a
divine presence in the world and to be known for its 'good
deeds' – all these are well attested NT themes common to 1
Peter and much of the epistolary literature of the NT.

What then is distinctive? This question was with us in the
beginning (see p. 89) and to it we return. The answer that
makes 1 Peter unusually serviceable to the church in later ages
begins with the obvious reminder that 1 Peter's first readers
were not members of the eyewitness generation (1 Pet. 1. 8,
12). They had not seen the Lord, as the authors claim for
themselves as they exploit their link with the apostle Peter (and
later on the same or similar Petrine group will do so again, 2
Pet. 1. 16–18). Yet there is no nostalgic looking back to
far-away days beyond recall. Instead 1 Peter enters the bold
claim that each generation is contemporary with the followers
of Jesus long ago – or, more theologically expressed, that the
living Lord is the guarantor of the tradition that stretches back
to its fountain-head and source. Hope is much more than
vague optimism that 'all shall be well and all manner of things
shall be well'; rather it is that virtue, along with faith (1. 21),
that pins us to the living Christ who is the same in every age.

This central motif of 'hope in Christ' is used to colour and
transform all life's relationships: to God as obedient children
and servants (1. 3, 17, 23; 2. 16), to church government and
organization (5. 1–5; a clear sign that these early communities
were becoming institutionalized yet without loss of charismatic
flexibility, 4. 10–11), to domestic affairs and household
management (3. 1–7; 2. 18–21), and to the wider ramifications

concludes: '1 Peter is the product of a Petrine tradition transmitted by Petrine
tradents of a Petrine circle' (*Perspectives*, 9).

of the church in secular society (2. 16–17). While 1 Peter does not explicitly remark on this, its ethos is that Christ's living presence is there in Pontus-Bithynia no less than in (say) Rome where Petrine influence is now becoming consolidated (1 Clement) or in Galilee from which the Petrine tradition originated as the memory and influence of the great apostle were cherished and preserved.

First Peter's chiefest contribution may well be the way we can see how apostolic authority in the hands of the apostles' successors was applied to churchly situations in far-flung outposts of the Roman Empire. Yet 'authority' is a slippery word, though its note does occur in this pastoral context (1. 1; 4. 11; 5. 1). Let us modify it by recalling Ignatius' dictum, 'Where Jesus Christ is, there is the catholic church' (*Smyr.* 8. 2), and by concluding that the presence of the victorious Lord is promised to all these early Bithynian communities needed to see them through their trials. The optimism of grace on which note 1 Peter closes (5. 10) is God's gift vouchsafed to the churches in the world of our day.

CHAPTER 7

2 Peter

THE OCCASION OF THE LETTER

The second epistle of Peter claims to be the work of the apostle under his Semitic name of Symeon (1. 1; 3. 1; as in Acts 15. 14) and to be written to a group of Christian believers of unknown origin (1. 1). One of the surest conclusions as to why the letter was composed is based on the evidence of 1. 13–15, according to which the writer viewed the approach of his death as a sign that he should leave his written testament for posterity. The purpose of writing is to alert the readers to the ideas and actions of false teachers whose presence and influence are already being felt (2. 1–3; 3. 3–7). For the most part the letter is polemical, with an argumentative thrust that is both direct (2. 1; 3. 3) and indirect (1. 16).[1] The author is moved by the situation to challenge, and respond to, teaching that he regards as erroneous (especially in ch. 3). At the same time the letter sets out a pattern of teaching by which the readers may remain faithful to the apostolic traditions of which Peter is regarded as the custodian. The call is therefore one of reminder and recall (1. 12–21; 3. 2), coupled with notes of instruction and caution.[2]

---

[1] As E. Fuchs remarks, *La deuxième épître de saint Pierre*, Neuchâtel/Paris 1980, 15.

[2] See C. H. Talbert, 'II Peter and the Delay of the Parousia', *Vigiliae Christianae* 20 (1966) 137–45 for this perceptive approach to 2 Peter. He notes the recurrent themes of 'remind' and 'understand' expressed as catchwords (1. 12, 13, 15; 3. 1–2 for the first verb; 'know' or 'understand' are found in 1. 20; 3. 3) and arranged in a way that divides the letter into two parts, 1. 3–2. 22 and 3. 1–18. 'Remind' is associated with the apostolic guarantee of the parousia and retribution, while 'understand' is linked with the prediction of the emergence of the false teachers (138–9).

Style and literary features

Of the 401 different words that are used in the composition of the letter, 57 are terms that appear nowhere else in the NT; 32 of those examples are not found in the entire Bible, and 11 of them could be designated rare words in the Greek language. Examples are words for 'vomit' (2. 22); 'rolling' in the mud (2. 22) in the proverb quoted; 'to be shortsighted' (1. 9); to throw down to Tartarus, the underworld in Greek mythology (2. 4), and 'false teachers' (2. 1).

At the opposite end of the spectrum of word usage, the author has a marked preference for certain words which he employs to great effect. Theological words like 'Lord' (15 times), 'God' (9 times), 'Jesus Christ' (9 times) are to be expected, given the nature of the writing as a Christian composition in epistolary form. Key words such as 'knowledge' (14 times), 'day' (12 times), 'righteous' (11 times) suggest the type of response he is making and the chief points of contention with the opposing teachers. Cosmological terms (like 'world', 'heaven[s]', 'water') and the vocabulary of salvation ('deliver' and its counterpart, 'destiny') are given ample prominence.

The lexical evidence is only part of the story. The author's style is carefully crafted, with rhetorical devices such as alliteration (2. 12; 3. 5) and assonance (2. 15–16 where *paranomia* ['transgression'] rhymes with *paraphronia* ['madness'] and a criss-cross arrangement of words to form a chiasmus (1. 12–21; 3. 2). The impression given is that of a writer who has access to an artificial dialect of high-sounding words learnt from rhetoricians or books, but used with a certain uneasiness associated with a style and language acquired in later life.[3] Other descriptions[4] of 2 Peter's word use and phraseology speak of its Asia Minor style (as different from a purer style of Attic Greek in the homeland), and its verbose and high-sounding manner of expression leaning towards the novel, the bizarre, and the use of coined words.

[3] J. H. Moulton and W. F. Howard, *A Grammar of New Testament Greek*, vol. 2, Edinburgh 1919, 28.
[4] B. Reicke, *The Epistles of James, Peter and Jude*. Anchor Bible 37, New York 1964, 146–7.

The literary structure of 2 Peter is even more elaborate than the use of rare and elevated terms might suggest.[5]

I. *Letter opening* (1. 1–2). The writer addresses his audience (not really defined) with words of commendation and prayer.

II. *Exordium* (1. 3–15). This section is part-homily (3–11), part-autobiography (12–15). The author is laying the groundwork for the body of his testamentary letter which is contained in 1. 16–3. 13.

III. *Probatio* (1. 16–3. 13). This is obviously the central core of 2 Peter in which a series of accusations is brought against the opponents and their claims refuted:

(i)   First indictment ('The hope of the parousia is a myth', 1. 16) refuted by 1. 16–19 with its double appeal to eyewitness testimony at the Transfiguration (16–18) and to the documentary evidence of the OT as understood in Peter's church (1. 19).

(ii) Second indictment ('The appeal to OT prophecy is vain', 1. 20–21) refuted by the double assertion that prophetic interpretation rests on *consensus fidelium*, not on one's private whim, and that OT prophets were spirit-inspired witnesses to the parousia (1. 21).

(iii) Third indictment, based on an exposure of the presence of false teachers who are branded as heretical, immoral, and yet influential within the congregation (2. 1–3). They are doomed to ruin (3), but they do not recognize this fate ('Divine judgment is not serious', 2. 3b; 3.9). This allegation is opposed by a long appeal to history which shows how the wicked are punished and the righteous vindicated – a sign that a future parousia will bring inevitable judgement and reward (2. 3–10).

(iv) A digression, with denunciations of the moral practices of the sectarians, partly drawn from Jude, partly based on proverbial wisdom (2. 10–22).

---

[5] See D. F. Watson, *Invention, Arrangement, and Style*. Rhetorical Criticism of Jude and 2 Peter. SBLDS 104, Atlanta 1988, 141–6.

(v) Fourth indictment and its refutation (3.1–13), commencing with a call to 'remember and understand' apostolic traditions and meeting the objection, 'The Parousia will not come since the first generation apostles are dead and there is no divine intervention in history' (3. 3–4) refuted by several lines of proof (3. 5–7) (a) the flood happened to validate God's word (3. 5–6); (b) the fire will burn up the old creation at the parousia (3. 7); (c) delay in the parousia is only relative to human and divine reckonings of time (3. 8); (d) delay is a gracious signal of divine forbearance (3. 9); (e) the apostolic teaching (in the gospel tradition) promises a parousia (3. 10).

(vi) Transition to moral application (3. 11–13) with calls to patience and holy living.

IV. *Peroratio* (3. 14–18). A miscellany of closing appeals directed to a moral call ('be at peace'), the authority of Paul in his letters, the warning note of error's pernicious ways – and rounded off with a summary prayer and doxology (3. 18).

Issues of authorship and dating

The document professes to be the work of 'Simon Peter, a servant and apostle of Jesus Christ' (1. 1). The author claims that he was an eyewitness of the Lord's Transfiguration (1. 16–18), though the plural verb-form (*'we were* eyewitnesses') is significant, as if to emphasize the apostolic nature of the testimony against those who followed humanly devised myths. He attests a relationship to Paul, his 'beloved brother' (3. 15) that appears to put his own authority on the same level as that of the apostle to the Gentiles. These two pieces of information have seemed compelling evidence to a few scholars that the letter is the work of the apostle Peter.[6]

---

[6] E. M. B. Green, *2 Peter Reconsidered*, London 1961, 36; cf. J. A. T. Robinson, *Redating to the New Testament*, London 1976, 175–84, who cites the concession of J. B. Mayor, *Jude and II Peter*, London 1907, 164–6 that 'the manner in which St. Paul is spoken of seems to me just what we should have expected from his brother Apostle'. Yet

But the issues are not so easily resolved, and most modern writers find counterbalancing evidence to point in the direction of (i) 2 Peter's origin in a later period than Peter's own lifetime (by tradition he was martyred in 65 CE) and (ii) its being the product of a group that revered his memory and used his name as authority and aegis to publish a tract that has a situation in view much later than the 60s.[7] The following items are the reasons for this confidence:

(i) The use made of the *letter of Jude*. Obviously there are strong verbal links between the two books as the following table will display:

Jude	2 Peter
4	2. 1–3
5	2. 5
6, 7	2. 4, 6
8, 9	2. 10, 11
10	2. 12
11–12	2. 15, 13
12–13	2. 17
16	2. 18
17	3. 2
18	3. 3

A tell-tale indication of the direction of indebtedness comes at Jude 12b–13 // 2 Peter 2. 17, where 'wandering stars' are consigned to the 'gloom of darkness' – a mixed metaphor in Jude that is cleared up in 2 Peter by likening the false teachers to 'clouds and mists' destined to disappear in the darkness.

The links with 1 Peter (as may be suspected from 3. 1) are not so clear, but they betray a shared tradition; both books have 153 words in common. Yet there are differences in

Mayor, who argues for the pseudonymity of the epistle, adds that 'this does not of course prove the genuineness of the present letter'.

[7] Most recently, R. J. Bauckham, *Jude and 2 Peter* WBC 50, Waco 1983, 327–30 who concludes that the author may have some personal connection with Peter, but not as a disciple. He was, Bauckham thinks, a senior member of the circle of church leaders at Rome when he wrote the letter as a 'testament of Peter' in the 80s – a conclusion now reinforced by Marion L. Soards, '1 Peter, 2 Peter, and Jude as Evidence for a Petrine School', *ANRW* 2/25, section 5, eds. W. Haase and H. Temporini (1985), 3827–49. On the issues of pseudonymity, see D. G. Meade, *Pseudonymity in the New Testament*, Tübingen/Grand Rapids 1986, and later, pp. 145–7.

nuance, as where 2 Peter uses *parousia* for the Lord's coming in glory, where 1 Peter prefers 'apocalypse'. The flood in Noah's time is used in 1 Peter 3. 20–1 as a type of baptism, whereas in 2 Peter 2. 5; 3. 5–7 it is a picture of cosmic destruction. This paradox of dissimilarity of style, yet with points of contact in the wording, would give added support to the following conclusions. The author of 2 Peter was a devoted member of the Petrine school. He knew traditions about the early Palestinian church and its connection with the Holy Family (hence acquaintance with Jude). And he was intent on assembling and publishing a testament to his teacher and his influence to meet a pressing need in his own day, now removed from the times of the apostles (3. 2; cf. 3. 4: 'since the fathers fell asleep' in death) who are appealed to as authority figures.

(ii) The *testamentary character* of 2 Peter is one of the clearest signs of its post-Petrine setting. In form 2 Peter is a farewell speech, based on Jewish (Jacob's speech in Gen. 47. 29–49. 28; Moses in Deut. 28–31; Joshua in Josh. 23–4; Samuel in 1 Sam. 12; Tobit in Tobit 14. 3–11 and the patriarchs in *Testaments of the Twelve Patriarchs*) and Christian models.[8] The latter category includes Jesus' final discourses (Mark 13 and par.; John 13–16) and Paul's valedictions in Acts 20. 18–35; 2 Timothy 3–4, and are particularly interesting. Several features recur in 2 Peter: the leaders are about to die (cf. Acts 20. 18–23, 25, 29, 38; 2 Tim. 4. 6–8); they predict the rise of heresy and a falling away after their demise (cf. Mark 13. 5–8, 22; Jn 16. 1, 32; Acts 20. 29–30; 2 Tim. 4. 3–4) and they appeal to personal/ apostolic example and instruction to safeguard the hearers against error or the abandonment of the faith (cf. Acts 20. 18–21, 27, 31, 33–5; 2 Tim. 3. 10; cf. 1 Tim. 1. 15; 2. 18). This literary format of 'discours d'adieu' has provided the author of 2 Peter with a model, using the example of the historical Peter who is said to be at the point of departure from life (1. 15) and whose constant appeal is to 'remembrance' and

---

[8] On this genre see J. Munck, 'Discours d'adieu dans le NT et la littérature biblique', *Aux sources de la tradition chrétienne*. Mélanges offert à M. Goguel, Neuchâtel 1950, 155–70.

'instruction' (1. 12, 13, 15; 3. 1–2) given as catchwords especially in 1. 3–2. 22; 3. 1–18.

The emergence of heresy on the scene, as we observed, is the occasion of the letter's writing; its tone and appeal reflect dependence on a now established literary convention to raise a bulwark against sectarian teaching and influence. This ploy suggests the work of a post-apostolic writer or school.

(iii) *The nature of the false teaching* is a matter for continuing and unresolved debate.[9] Yet there seems to be a consensus, even if the use of terms like 'gnostic' is in dispute, that a serious threat to the apostolic teaching and way of life was present. Strong language (in 2. 1) is used of those who sponsor 'pernicious heresies' (cf. NEB, 'disruptive views', JB is a shade weak: the 'views' are more like 'doctrines', so Fuchs,[10] appealing to Ignatius, *Ephesians* 6. 2; *Trallians* 6. 1; Justin, *Dialogue* 51. 2). As with the case of the problems faced in Jude's letter the ideas he opposes are both doctrinal and ethical. Second Peter's opponents cherish a cavalier attitude to angelic powers (2. 10), and they are deemed to be anti-Christ (2. 1). Their moral influence, for the author, is deleterious in the extreme, chiefly in their promoting and practice of the slogan given out in 2. 19: 'Freedom from corruption' – a promise that the author of 2 Peter turns on its head. They are veritable slaves of corruption, whereas true freedom is gained only by sharing in God's nature (1. 4) and by living a godly life (1. 5–11; 3. 14).

The teachers appear to have been successful, more so than in the earlier situation of Jude's writing. The readers are in danger of 'falling away' (1. 10), 'being exploited' (2. 3) and 'enticed' (2. 14) into an apostasy (3. 17). Hence the stringent warnings issued in Peter's name. And the opponents' appeal was evidently reinforced by their several-pronged accusation brought against the church leaders (see the analysis, pp. 136–7). In particular they denied the reality of judgement, and pre-

---

[9] The fullest survey in English is by Thomas S. Caulley, 'The False Teachers in Second Peter', *Studia Biblica et Theologica* 12/1 (1982) 27–42, with bibliography. Cf. H. C. C. Cavallin, 'The False Teachers of 2 Peter as Pseudo-Prophets', *NovT* 21 (1979) 263–70.

[10] E. Fuchs, *La deuxième épître de saint Pierre*, 78.

ferred an idiosyncratic interpretation of OT prophecy, pointing to the passing of the apostolic generation as proof that 'prophecy doesn't work' in its predictive role. Above all, the teachers poured scorn on the futurity of the parousia on the ground that the apostolic tradition that took its stand on the Lord's word to come again was falsified by history and that the course of history flows on in imperturbably smooth channels, with no divine interposition. The delay in the parousia was thus the major buttress to support and defend their beliefs and behaviour.

The expectation that Christ would come 'soon', presumably in the generation then living, is amply attested in all parts of the NT literature. There are 'sayings of Jesus' preserved in the Synoptic Gospels that hold out the hope of some kind of immediate return or reappearance of the Son of man to his disciples (Matt. 10. 23) or an appearance of Christ in the lifetime of the hearers (Mark 9. 1; 13. 30). At Thessalonica, it was understood from some earlier Pauline instruction that the parousia was soon to happen, bringing with it the wind up of history (1 Thess. 4. 13–5. 11). Paul can elsewhere place himself with those who will be 'still alive' when the Lord appears from heaven (1 Cor. 15. 51), and he can write about the time of the end being 'near' (1 Cor. 7. 26, 29), a hope shared in the Revelation of John (Rev. 1. 3, 7; 22. 12–17, 20).

When the parousia did not take place with such speed, it naturally raised all manner of questions and doubts and posed some theological problems in 2 Peter to which we will return (pp. 156, 159–60). At Corinth the future hope became 'collapsed' into present experience and one's baptism was regarded as ushering in the new age in its fullness (1 Cor. 4. 8; 15. 12). Deaths in the congregation would have to be accounted for realistically (1 Cor. 11. 30–2; cf. 1 Thess. 4. 13), as later the passing of the generation of the first apostles posed its own problems (Jn. 21. 20–3). Partial solutions were found in Paul's understanding of the tension between what is now (we are saved by Christ's death and resurrection and have the Spirit as a first instalment, 2 Cor. 1. 22; Rom. 8. 23) and what is still set in the future, at the parousia to come (1 Cor. 11. 26; 15. 23, 50–7): the final kingdom of God destined to take over from the interim 'reign of Christ' (1 Cor. 15. 20–8). John's solution lies in the promise that the parousia in some sense has already occurred in Christ's return to the Father and the gift of the Spirit to the church (Jn. 14. 21, 28; 16. 5–10, 16). Luke's Acts (in 1. 4–11) tries to combine the two ideas of Christ's presence in the coming of the Spirit (1. 8) and the cherished belief that the Lord will return in person (1. 11). It is left to 2 Peter to offer the fullest rationale for the delay of the parousia hope (2 Pet. 3. 3–9): that delay does not imply denial since ideas of time are not the same with God as with mortals, and in the waiting period God is gracious to allow space for repentance.

But it is difficult to see these arguments as satisfying 2 Peter's opponents who appealed to their immediate experience as rendering the thought of a future coming unnecessary. They appear to have stressed the reality of salvation here and now, introducing them to a life where the claims of morality were dismissed once their 'spirits' were joined to God's life and they shared in his nature (see 1. 4; 2. 12 as Peter's response). With the resurrection already past (2 Tim. 2. 18) they imagined themselves beyond the range of morality since there was no prospect of judgement and accountability for deeds done in this life. This outlook is evident at Corinth (1 Cor. 4. 1–5; 5. 6–8; 15. 32–4) and it represents a major shift in the eschatological debate underlying 2 Peter.

The search for a suitable *Sitz im Leben* for teaching in the developed form it has in 2 Peter invites comparison with two or possibly three sets of documents ranging from near the close of the first Christian century to the mid-second century.[11] The texts in question begin with 1 Clement (*c.* 96 CE) which has some vague allusions to libertine ethics (28. 1–30. 8; 33. 1–2; 35. 1–12; 37. 1–2) alongside a denial of resurrection-to-judgement (24. 1–5; 26. 1–3) with the clearest parallel in 1 Clement 23. 3–4 which reflects the same disillusion over the parousia hope that lies behind 2 Peter 3. 1–3. In both docu-

---

[11] Cf. C. H. Talbert, 'II Peter and the Delay of the Parousia', 144–5; T. S. Caulley, 'The False Teachers', 40–2.

ments it is reaffirmed that delay does not betoken denial, for 'he shall come quickly and will not delay' (cf. Heb. 10. 37).

The letter of Polycarp to the Philippians is more immediately relevant, for here we come across a bold assertion that 'the sayings of the Lord' are being twisted to deny both resurrection and judgement:

For 'whosoever does not confess that Jesus Christ is come in the flesh is antichrist' [cf. 2 Pet. 2. 1] ... and whosoever perverts the sayings of the Lord to suit his own lusts [cf. 2 Pet. 3. 3, 16] and says there is neither resurrection nor judgment – such a one is the first-born of Satan. (Phil. 7. 1)

Polycarp's response to this aberration is to recall the apostolic tradition, which he uses to refute these denials of Jesus' full humanity, the reality of his crucifixion, and the prospect of parousia-judgement: 'Let us turn back to the word delivered to us from the beginning' (7. 2) – a striking similarity to the appeal 2 Peter makes to the authoritative apostolic tradition and testimony.

The third parallel text is from the Epistle to Rheginos in the Nag Hammadi collection.

The Savior swallowed death ... He raised Himself up (having 'swallowed' the visible by means of the invisible), and gave us the way to our immortality. So then as the Apostle said of Him, we have suffered with Him, and arisen with Him and ascended into heaven with Him ... This is the resurrection of the spirit, which 'swallows up' resurrection of the soul along with the resurrection of the flesh. (*Gnostic Treatise on the Resurrection: Epistle to Rheginos*, 44. 46–45. 68)

This text is one of the clearest assertions of a spiritualized resurrection, replacing the Pauline doctrine of 1 Corinthians 15.[12]

It is impossible to conclude with any degree of certainty that these three texts and 2 Peter all belong to the same specific tendency, but there are common features in evidence to allow a hypothesis. This proposal is to the effect that somewhere in the

---

[12] On this see K. Koschorke, 'Paulus in den Nag-Hammadi-Texten', *ZTK* 78 (1981) 177–205; E. H. Pagels, *The Gnostic Paul: Gnostic Exegesis of the Pauline Letters*, Philadelphia, 1975.

range of *c.* 100–150 CE (a broad spectrum!) the orthodox tradition, represented in 1 Clement and Polycarp had to confront head-on an errant teaching that gathered to itself many facets. The chiefest of these was a device used to explain the non-occurrence of the parousia with a consequent devaluing of the apostolic witness to Christ and the end of history. At its heart was a development of the move made at Corinth to place the heart-beat of the Christian faith in the risen Christ and the fullness of the new age in him here and now – with a resultant downplaying of his human nature, and of the centrality of the cross as both atoning and exemplary with a call to 'die to self and sin'. There followed a sidelining of the hope of the parousia with its attendant insistence on moral accountability at the future judgement.

The author of 2 Peter makes his counter-claim on the basis of Peter the apostle whose role was that of the guardian of the orthodox faith. Peter had successfully overcome rivals in his lifetime (notably in Acts 8. 9–25) and Simon Magus became the archetype of false teaching and the father of Gnosticism in the later church (Irenaeus, *Against All Heresies* 1. 23, 3f.). So the Petrine tradition harks back to the patronage of Peter whose testament it seeks to use in repelling dangerous doctrines and antinomian practices in later decades.

(iv) A final observation shows how the interpretation of scripture – both the Lord's oracles and the apostles' testimony – could become the centre of controversy. The opponents' claim to be true exponents of scripture, or to set aside the orthodox views of scripture regarding prophecy, lies behind much of the inferred dialogue in the background of 2 Peter. Hence we hear the counter-argument in 1. 19–21; 2. 21; 3. 14–18. Of especial interest is the use made of Paul's epistles, now evidently regarded by both parties as a collection and as replete with authority. The 'orthodox' author of 2 Peter professes a warm attachment to Paul in his own person (3. 15) and looks to him to support his case against those who as 'ignorant and unstable' teachers twist Paul's letters to their own ruin 'as they do the other scriptures'. This is one of the clearest signs of a setting for 2 Peter in a period when Paul's letters are already

assembled (note 'all his letters'), are the object of study (as in
Polycarp, *Phil.* 3. 2), and are accorded a status and authority
close to what we mean today by 'canonical'. The recourse to
Paul's epistles is the writer's strategy which would only be
available to him long after Paul's death and the bringing
together of his correspondence into a unity – at a time when it
was also possible to speak of 'your apostles' (3. 2) in reflection
on the now closed apostolic era (cf. Ignatius, *Rom.* 4. 2–3: 'I do
not give you orders like Peter and Paul. They were apostles; I
am a convict').

The document known as 2 Peter carries marks of having
been composed by members of the 'school of Peter' (see earlier
pp. 90–4) at a time when Peter's memory was cherished and his
aegis claimed for teaching required to repel rival teachers. The
letter, then, even more clearly than 1 Peter, is a pseudonym.
That is, it uses the name and authority of the chief apostle to
convey teaching that his followers believed was in keeping with
his abiding influence and continuing spirit in the churches
(presumably those founded by him).

This procedure is parallel with the way the influence of the
Hebrew prophets lived on in the writings of their disciples (see
Isa. 8. 16) or the teachings of Socrates and Plato were imitated
in the later philosophical schools.

There is no pretence involved, which would be the case if the
letter was passed off as a supposedly genuine composition,
making it a forgery. Nor was there, so far as we can tell, an
intention to hoodwink the readers. (Hence modern scholars are
questioning whether 'pseudonym' is the best word to use.[13])
Rather, nobler motives were at work. Not least among which is
the conviction that the apostle's name could legitimately be
used because he was believed to be living in heaven and
speaking to the contemporary situation through his devoted

---

[13] As K. Koch remarks, 'Since what is involved is not the conscious use of an
inaccurate name, the designation "pseudonymous" should be used only with
reservations', *Interpreter's Dictionary of the Bible.* Supplementary Volume, Nashville
1976, 713. A change of nomenclature may help to deflect some of the criticisms
brought by E. E. Ellis, 'Pseudonymity and Canonicity of NT Documents', in: M. J.
Wilkins and T. Paige (eds.), *Worship, Theology and Ministry in the Early Church*,
Sheffield 1992, JSNTSS 87, 212–24.

friends and followers. In this way to call on the name of an honoured leader like Peter (presumably now having received a martyr's crown) was tantamount to professing belief in the continuing activity of the Holy Spirit and ascribing the writing to God as ultimate author – a point that is expressly made in our letter (2 Pet. 1. 19–21).

Summary

In the NT book of 2 Peter we have to do with an elaborately constructed polemic document. Drawing on traditions that flow from many sources – mainly the report of the Lord's oracles and the apostles' tradition, the data garnered from early Palestinian Christianity found in the letter of Jude, and a deposit of revered memory and instruction linked with Peter's name, the representatives of Petrine orthodoxy (at Rome?) published a tract aimed at repelling antinomian 'gnosticizing' error in the churches. The document thus raises a bulwark of opposition to what are deemed heretical positions and persuasions which seemed to have had some success. The basis for this countermeasure is the apostolic tradition and the church's interpretation of scripture, including the Pauline epistles, with a double exhortation: to recall what the apostles taught and left as their legacy, and to be instructed by their example and influence claimed to be present in their (true) successors.

BACKGROUNDS TO THE THEOLOGICAL CONTRIBUTIONS OF 2 PETER

2 Peter as a NT book under suspicion

In the esteem of many readers 2 Peter stands on the fringe of the New Testament. Its claim to be heard as an authentic witness to Christ and his way is muffled and indistinct. When issues about whether the NT canon is 'closed', and what makes a document part of 'holy scripture' or an authentic Christian source-book are discussed, 2 Peter is often cited as a candidate for rejection,[14] with ready replacements such as Ignatius' letters or the Epistle to Diognetus waiting in the wings.

The status of 2 Peter as part of the NT canon with normative value is both an ancient and a modern challenge. First, we look at the way the letter struggled to gain acceptance among the early canon-makers; then we survey the recent debate which centres on the label 'early Catholic' as applied to 2 Peter. Only when these matters are before us will we be in a position to assess 2 Peter's theological value(s).

Historical attestation

2 Peter had a slow, cautious and sporadic reception into the church's canon, or list of authoritative books. In the second century the book is known among some second-century writers with the clearest evidence in the *Apocalypse of Peter* (*c.* 110–40 CE) which has a few verbal parallels to the text of 2 Peter. But the evidence otherwise is sparse and disputed, leading to the conclusion that 2 Peter was not in general use. The *Acts of Peter* (*c.* 180 CE) bears witness to 2 Peter's existence, and in Justin, *Dialogue* 82. 1 there is a probable allusion to 2 Peter 2. 1.

The association with the apostle Peter whose name appears in the book makes the scarcity of explicit references to 2 Peter a problem; it is not until Origen – or at least his friend and pupil Firmilian (Eusebius, *Church History* Bk. 6, ch. 27, section 1) that there is specific mention of the letter as linked with Peter (according to Cyprian, *Ep.* 75. 6). Origen (*Commentary on John* 5. 3) speaks of one acknowledged letter 'and, it may be a second one, for it is doubted'. In Eusebius' list (*Church History* Bk. 3, ch. 3, sections 1–4; cf. 25. 3) 2 Peter is classed with the 'disputed books' (*antilegomena*). This judgement is expressed by Didymus the Blind (died 398 CE) who left to history the apparently unequivocal verdict: 'it is therefore not to be

---

[14] E. Käsemann, 'The New Testament Canon and the Unity of the Church', *Essays on New Testament Themes*, London 1964, 95–107.

overlooked that the present epistle is forged [*esse falsatum*] which, though it is read publicly [in the churches], is nevertheless not in the canon' (*Patrologia Latina* 39, col. 1742). Yet discoveries in 1941 in Toura, south of Cairo, reveal a group of codices on papyrus (6th–7th century) containing the text of a half-dozen additional commentaries of Didymus of Alexandria in which he quotes from 2 Peter as authentic or authoritative.[15]

The ominous note of 'forgery' is sounded in this witness, and Eusebius' later reference mentioned above (*Church History* Bk. 3, ch. 25, section 3) puts 2 Peter with other books 'to be spoken against' (*antilegomena*).

Modern doubts

This tale of uncertainty and doubt was reinforced in the Reformation period. One reformer Oecolampadius (1482–1531) speaks for his generation to the effect that the Reformers accepted all twenty-seven books of the NT, but at the same time 'we do not compare the Apocalypse, along with ... 2 Peter ... with the rest of the books' (*Epistolarum libri quattuor*, Basle 1536, 31). This notion of books that belong to a central core-canon and others (like 2 Peter, Jude, Jas., 1–2 Jn., Rev.) that are pushed out to the periphery has played a significant part in the recent understanding of 2 Peter as only secondary in its witness to Christ.

E. Käsemann[16] has launched an attack on 2 Peter by dubbing it an 'early catholic' work, i.e. in Käsemann's terminology a NT book that fails to express the heart of the (Pauline) gospel and represents an accommodation of Christianity to hellenistic culture and categories. Marks of 'early catholic' influence are (i) a fading of the parousia hope as part of a general reordering of eschatological conviction seen in a demoting of Christ in the scenario, with a concentration of moralistic ideas. (ii) Ecclesiastical orders and offices are a second mark of the church's increasing bureaucratic control, seen in 1 Clement

---

[15] B. M. Metzger, *The Canon of the New Testament*, Oxford 1987, 213.

[16] E. Käsemann, 'An Apologia for Primitive Christian Eschatology', in *Essays on New Testament Themes*, London 1964, 169–95, especially 179–85, 193.

44 and the Ignatian epistles. (iii) The way in which the Christian faith is codified in set forms and fixed formulas leads to the setting up of a 'formal principle' of canonical authority as a bulwark against gnostic heresy. Christian doctrine is objectified and thereby a church of *beati possidentes* ('happy possessors'), who rejoice in their 'orthodoxy', replaces the earlier Christian charismatic groups, in which the sense of living in the fresh dawn of the new age and its fulfilment was strong and vivid.

Judged by these criteria, Käsemann asserts,[17] 2 Peter shows clear signs of its second-century setting. He argues that it wrestles with the non-imminence of the parousia and marks a recasting of eschatology to fit in with the world's indefinite continuance; that the church's role as a bastion of orthodoxy to counter 'false teachers' (2. 1) shows a distinct shift from Paul's ecclesiology of the church as charismatically moved and led. The church as guardian of scripture (in 1. 12–21; 3. 16) is said to betoken a teaching office held in honour against Paul's view (1 Cor. 12) that teaching and revelation are the dynamic possession of all the Spirit-gifted members of the congregation; and that faith (*pistis*) in 2 Pet. 1. 5–7 (cf. Jude 3, 20: see earlier p. 77) has lost its eschatological and existential character and signifies either one 'virtue' among many in the moral life or else the corpus of Christian belief as 'orthodox doctrinal tradition'. The upshot is that in 2 Peter the essential gospel, what Käsemann calls the 'material principle' (justification by faith), has been overlaid and corrupted. The witness of 2 Peter is not to the gospel, but to its transformation from 'event' to 'doctrine'. 2 Peter, then, for one compelling reason is to be discounted in the theological contribution it is said to offer. That contribution is a negative one, which is what happens when the 'material principle' is lost or replaced.

There is, in Käsemann's estimate, both truth and exaggeration. He has overstated the case in several ways, chiefly in ignoring the fact that the denial of imminence in the parousia

---

[17] E. Käsemann, 'Paul and Early Catholicism', in *New Testament Questions of Today*, London 1969, 236–7.

hope is the sectarians' position, not the author's. The latter has a strongly held belief in Christ's coming to judgement in apocalyptic glory (1. 19; 2. 12; 3. 10–14). He expresses Christian salvation in a way that sets a gulf between God's nature (as divine) and human existence (as mortal). As human beings are by definition 'weak', both physically and morally, and are the victims of impulses to error and wrongdoing, they should seek 'salvation' in what will answer these needs. God's divine power (1. 3) steps in to match such needs, and offers the promise of incorruption and moral strength (see 2. 19–20). Some interpreters have seen this as dualism setting an unbridgeable gap between God and humankind living in an evil world, and paving the way for later church teaching on 'divinization'.

The fourth-century Greek fathers went back to pseudo-Athanasius who remarked, 'The Son of God became son of man so that the sons of men ... might become sons of God ... partakers of the life of God.' Later Cyril of Alexandria wrote similarly, 'We are made partakers of the divine nature ... [and] are actually called divine ... because we have God dwelling in us'. The Cappadocian fathers framed a doctrine of salvation that consisted of mortals' sharing in God's life with the result of their becoming 'deified' (the Greek is *theopoiēsis*, 'made as God').[18] This teaching picks up the idiom of 2 Pet. 1. 4, from which developed an elaboration of the way human redemption is understood in eastern Christianity and the orthodox church: supreme blessedness is being made one with God – a goal powerfully aided by sacramental action, both in baptism and the Eucharist.[19]

We may question whether such development is implicit in 2 Peter's thought, given the polemical use of language which may well have been influenced by the opponents', an observation to which we return later (see p. 161) when we consider the theology underlying such a statement as in 1. 4.

The author of 2 Peter does have recourse to apostolic tradi-

[18] J. N. D. Kelly, *Early Christian Doctrines*, London 1958, 348–52.
[19] The 'change' (Gr. *metaballein*) in the eucharistic elements is given a saving value, parallel with the 'transformation' of the human condition to share the divine life. See J. R. Srawley, *The Early History of the Liturgy*, 2nd edn., London 1947, 222–4.

tions as the ground of appeal – here Käsemann's point is well taken – and this feature marks the normative character assigned to these apostolic 'words' (2. 21; 3. 2) and 'ways' (2. 1, 15, 21), yet they are not connected firmly to any apostolic office (except at 3. 2). Rather the entire audience of the letter is expected to react to its teaching and to interpret scripture for itself, much as in the Pauline congregations (1. 19–21; 3. 14–18). The author is building his case on apostolic testimony inherited from Peter and the apostles and adapting it to a post-Petrine situation. As Bauckham remarks,[20] this is the key to the author's conception of his task.

Finally, while 'faith' may have this nuance of *fides quae creditur* (see earlier p. 76), other Christian categories such as 'knowledge' are not so much 'orthodox doctrinal tradition' in 1. 2, 8 (so Käsemann) as a living relationship to Jesus Christ implied in personal conversion, as in Phil. 3. 7–10, etc.

Summary

To the extent that 2 Peter is a specimen of testamentary literature which, looking back to the historical Peter as its authority, addresses a later situation in categories that meet the need of the day, and relies on apostolic traditions and correctly interpreted scripture, the document belongs to a sub-apostolic age. Yet that is not the era of 'incipient catholicism' as seen in 1 Clement and Ignatius. The challenge to the orthodox faith may belong to the same time period, as we noted earlier, but the way in which the challenge is met is not the same. Rather than an appeal to institutionalized Christianity, 2 Peter still retains its roots with the vibrant apostolic communities.[21] It represents a strategy for coping with heresy that retains much of an eschatological–existential formulation that still centres in Christ, 'Lord and Saviour' (1. 1, 11; 2. 20; 3. 2, 18) as the locus and ground of salvation and cosmic hope, as Paul had maintained in his kerygma (3. 15–16).

[20] R. J. Bauckham, *Jude, 2 Peter* WBC 50, Waco 1983, 153.
[21] J. H. Elliott, 'A Catholic Gospel: Reflections on "Early Catholicism" in the New Testament', *CBQ* 31 (1969) 213–23.

THEOLOGICAL THEMES

Setting

With features that bind it more to Jude than to 1 Peter, this letter presents itself as expressing a number of distinctive theological features. It shares much of the apocalyptic world-view belonging to Jude, though its opponents are not quite the same. In Jude the false teachers were itinerant prophetic types who infiltrated the congregation with a rival message of 'salvation' that Jude saw as none other than an invitation to antinomian licence. Their ground of authority was evidently a charismatic awareness that overrode the apostolic traditions and 'faith' (3, 20). Jude denied this claim by branding it as 'not-of-the-spirit' (19).

In 2 Peter the opponents are less well defined. They share much of the same condemnation for their immoral ways and influence (2. 1–3, 10–22), and their catchwords (2. 19) were 'freedom' and 'no fear of future judgment'. They showed no respect for the angels (2. 10) and they openly paraded their supposed immunity from moral evil (2. 10, 13–14). Like Balaam (quoted in Jude 11; cf. Rev. 2. 14) their mercenary motives are exposed, as part of a standard, stock-in-trade denunciation of opponents.

The absence of any systematic dualism has led some scholars (Fornberg,[22] Neyrey,[23] Bauckham[24]) to insist that the opponents are not 'gnostic' – a slippery term, as we observed in the case of Jude. A lot depends on how the term is used, and we may grant the point that anything approaching the gnostic systems developed in the later second century is hardly the setting of 2 Peter (in spite of the reference to 'myths' in 1. 16, which may have more of a moral than a metaphysical quality:

[22] T. Fornberg, *An Early Church in a Pluralistic Society. A Study of 2 Peter*. Coniectanea Biblica. NT series 9, Uppsala, 1977.

[23] J. H. Neyrey, *The Form and Background of the Polemic in 2 Peter*, Yale, unpublished dissertation, 1977. The substance of Neyrey's work is in his article with the same title as above, *JBL* 99 (1980) 407–31.

[24] R. J. Bauckham, *Jude, 2 Peter* and his contribution to *ANRW* 2/25, section 5, '2 Peter: An Account of Research', 3713–52 (with bibliography).

see Fuchs[25]). If, as we argued, the root problem arose from a false conception of Christian salvation in which future hope was eliminated in a concentration on present experience, then this feature would account for the impunity with which the opponents defy moral claims and assert that the world goes on its way with no prospect of a day of accountability. This seems to be exactly in the background of their rationale in 3. 3–13. 2 Peter seeks to refute it by appealing to the orthodox Christian eschatology of both a final wind-up to history and a reminder of judgement to come.

Themes

Within the general framework of polemic and apologetic against this setting, 2 Peter's author sets out his basic convictions, which may be tabulated thus.

God as creator.

In the OT tradition of belief in one God, maker of heaven and earth, 2 Peter proclaims that the universe came into existence by divine fiat (3. 5, a verse that confronts directly the cosmology of the opponents: they overlook the fact that creation arose by the divine word that separated the seas from the earth according to Gen. 1. 9–10, as part of God's overall design). Unlike the point made in Hebrews 11. 3, 2 Peter wants to move on to that part of the creation story where earth and seas are distinguished in order that he may enforce his point concerning divine judgement by water (Gen. 7. 10, 12–13) in 3. 6. Noah's flood, for him, was no natural phenomenon, but a divine act (2. 5) wrought by the same powerful word that brought creation into being (Gen. 1).

From this position he goes on to establish his polemical arguments that (i) the present world-order (3. 7) is destined for God's judgement with adverse results for the 'godless' (i.e. his opponents), but (ii) the promise of a new creation, drawn from Isaiah 65. 17; 66. 22, is equally certain and is held out for the

25 E. Fuchs, *La deuxième épître*, 67.

reassurance of his readers. If the opponents are wilfully ignorant of past history (3. 5), the audience 2 Peter addresses are not in that state. Reminded with warm terms like 'beloved', they are not to ignore the future purposes of God for the cosmos (3. 8–10). Utilizing Psalm 90. 4 the writer builds on the divine character of 'timelessness' which he offers to justify what his opponents think of as 'delay' and 'neglect'. The non-intervention of God must not be held to betray God's weakness; rather he holds back the day of judgement ('the Day of Yahweh' originates in Amos 5. 18–20 as a time of reckoning for the nations, not rejoicing as was popularly thought in the prophet's time) as a sign of his patience and his love. Yet when the dread day does arrive, it will come suddenly 'like a thief' in the night to attack the unsuspecting household (a Palestinian image, Matt. 6. 19; 24. 43 and parallels (in other gospels) which found a place in later NT apocalyptic warnings, 1 Thess. 5. 2, 4; Rev. 3. 3; 16. 15; cf. 1 Clem. 23. 5). It will also herald the birth of a new cosmic order by dissolving the existing order with a 'mighty fracas' (Fuchs' term to bring out the onomatopoetic force of Peter's verb, rendered in 3. 10, NIV, 'with a roar') and a fiery dispersing of the 'elements' (*stoicheia*: a scientific term in Greek physics for the main components of matter). Out of such an explosive intervention in the cosmic structure, 2 Peter predicts, all things will be exposed in their true light and brought to judgement (the textual reading in 3. 10 is uncertain).

Yet the ultimate goal of this destructive work is optimistic as 2 Peter picks up the thought, common in some parts of Jewish apocalyptic writings, that God's purpose is to restore creation to its pristine beauty and harmony. This hope of 'restitution' (Gr. *apokatastasis*), in which eschatological expectation turns on a recovery of cosmic conditions as they were 'in the beginning', is at the heart of Origen's thought. The final restoration, which Origen based on 1 Cor. 15. 25–8, that all things will at the last be brought in subjection to God the creator, holds out the promise of universal salvation, though Origen stopped short of that conclusion. It is significant that the line of thinking stemming from 2 Peter to Origen offered an alternative to

the millenarianism that is found in the majority of the second-
and third-century writers, especially Irenaeus and Papias.
They thought in terms of the literal fulfilment of Jewish prophecies of miraculous prosperity and fecundity in the fields and
orchards, and Christ's literal reign for a thousand years while
Satan is bound (based on Rev. 20. 2–5). Not all the fathers
followed this literalistic line; Hippolytus gave a symbolic significance to the number 'one thousand' and yet he still clings to
the idea of an earthly rule of Christ, unlike the scenario in 2
Peter which Origen develops.

The fire is intended as a destructive agent (as in 3. 12), but
also as a symbolic prelude to the ushering in of a new cosmos
where righteousness will have its home. The severely negative
images of judgement and ruin leading to cosmic destruction
give way to a new role set for God the creator. He will create
afresh, and the next time his work will be qualitatively better –
'new heavens and new earth' – because it will be free from the
ungodliness that so vexed the righteous soul of 2 Peter's hero,
Lot (2. 7). The application to the readers' situation follows on
immediately (3. 14–15) with calls to faithful living and moral
blamelessness, framed by the *inclusio*-device that brings
together God's patience in withholding retribution (3. 9) and
God's patience in proffering salvation (3. 15). The circle is
complete.

God as judge.
The fiercely worded sentence of doom on the sinful world arose
directly out of the scoffers' excuse that (i) the coming of the
Lord is delayed (3. 3) and (ii) the course of history flows
without interruption or break (3. 4). The first generation of
Christians has come and gone, and there is no hint of any
fulfilment of prophetic catastrophe (3. 4). For 2 Peter this
sceptical attitude is not the outcome of neutral observation, but
evinces an ungodly disposition that turns away from the apostolic teaching which derives from the Lord's own 'commandment' (cf. 2. 21 which shows how the idea of transmission of a
'holy word' from its source in the Lord to the churches via 'the
apostles' was conceived). In particular, the scoffers are

branded as 'indulging their own lusts' (3. 3), which puts a moral label on their error. For that reason, 2 Peter bears down on his opponents as people liable to divine judgement and destruction.

In ch. 2 the judgement-theme is displayed in a set of panels where the 'false teachers' (2. 1) are no better than the 'false prophets' of ancient Israel, apocalyptic Judaism, and early Christian predictions of end-times that are already begun (Matt. 7. 15; 1 Jn. 4. 1; 1 Tim. 4. 1–4; and, for apocalyptic scenes, see Matt. 24. 11, 24; Mark 13. 22). Three traits are spelled out as branding them as 'false':

(i) They introduce false teaching (2. 1) and do so furtively (cf. Gal. 2. 4 of 'false brothers' who 'secretly' slipped in to the Pauline churches). 2 Peter's false teachers 'deny' the Lord who saves his people either by renouncing him (Matt. 10. 33 // Luke 12. 9; Jn. 13. 38; 18. 27; 2 Tim. 2. 12; Rev. 2. 13; 3. 8) or, more likely, by their attitude to him and his parousia they abandon his teaching and deny the faith as scoffers (3. 3) or as blasphemers (2. 2; cf. *Apocalypse of Peter* 21 for a clear reference to this verse). We may compare 1 Timothy 5. 8; 2 Timothy 3. 5; Titus 1. 16; 1 John 2. 22–3; Hermas, *Similitudes* 8. 8. 4 for a renunciation of Christian belief and profession.

(ii) They attract to themselves a considerable following (2. 2) from among the faithful, and encourage them in licentious ways (as in Jude 4) – a sexually oriented allusion as is clear from 2. 7, 18.

(iii) They are governed by love of money (2. 3), with the twin features of inordinate greed for gain (Gr. *pleonexia*) and a policy of milking the congregations by commercial exploitation (Gr. *emporeuesthai*; cf. the verb in Jas. 4. 13).

On all counts they are ripe for judgement.

God's juridical act is introduced at 2. 4 and the argument follows an orderly pattern. Building on the assertion in 2. 3 – a kind of thesis that 'judgment is inevitable' – the author proceeds to illustrate from past historical examples (2. 4, 5, 6). The antithesis comes in 5, 7–8 as past examples of deliverance (Noah, Lot) act as a foil to the dark side of judgement. Then, at 9 a type of synthesis recalls both the thesis and the antithesis, to complete the movement of thought.

Judgement falls on the unbelieving godless as 2 Peter uses a miscellany of picturesque descriptions of celebrated cases of judgement and deliverance in the past:

(i) Angels who sinned (Gen. 6. 1–4) are consigned to the prison underworld of Tartarus, the lowest region of the classical Hades; it is used as a place of punishment in 1 Enoch 20. 2, as elsewhere Job 41. 24 (LXX); Philo, *De Praemiis et Poenis* 152; Josephus, *Against Apion* 2. 240; *Sibylline Oracles* 4. 186. They are consigned to dark caverns (reinterpreting Jude 6) and they are reserved for a sentence of retribution (*Jubilees* 5, 6, 10; 1 Enoch 10. 4–6).

(ii) Next is introduced the world of the Flood (Gen. 6. 11–9. 17) which not only follows on the story of the Heavenly Watchers in Gen. 6. 1–4, but is closely linked with that event, so that in 1 Enoch the second (Flood) is the direct consequence of the first (merging of the sexes in Gen. 6). Divine judgement came with the flood as the ancient world was submerged (2. 5; 3. 6); 2 Peter sees in this world a picture of the moral universe around him (1. 4; 2. 20; 3. 7); and there needs to be destruction and a new beginning made (3. 13). The believers who are to guard themselves from evil stain (1. 4; 2. 20; 3. 14) are typified in Noah whose chief characteristic was his 'righteousness', the possession of Peter's faithful church (1. 1). But the main interest lies in assertion of the notes of judgement on Noah's generation, held to be the worst case of sinners imaginable (cf. 1 Pet. 3. 20; see Mishnah, *Sanhedrin* 10. 3). The false teachers evidently thought, like Noah's contemporaries, that judgement was 'idle' and God was 'asleep' – and they need to be alert to the contrary as a warning of their peril. God is still merciful in his forbearance (3. 9, 15) as the next illustration shows.

(iii) Righteous Lot (Gen. 19. 30–8) is here painted in better colours than in the Genesis account. Rabbinic pictures[26] of him make him more of a symbolic sinner, but occasionally (Wis.

---

[26] R. J. Bauckham, 'James, 1 and 2 Peter, Jude', in: D. A. Carson and H. G. M. Williamson (eds.), *It is Written: Scripture Citing Scripture*, Fest. B. Lindars. Cambridge 1988, especially 314–15. See too S. Rappaport, 'Der gerechte Lot', *ZNW* 29 (1930) 299–304.

Sol. 10. 6; 19. 17) he is called a 'religious' or 'righteous' person (cf. 1 Clem. 11. 1) in contrast to the ungodly inhabitants of the Cities of the Plain (in 2. 6) whose time for destruction came in its season much like the argument in Sirach 16. 6–14. The tragic circumstances of this judgement on Sodom and Gomorrah is a frequent theme in both Jewish and Christian proclamation. The totality of the destruction makes the rescue of Lot all the more impressive, and 2 Peter's purpose is to mark the vast distinction between righteous Lot and the lawless Sodomites (2. 7). He builds on Jude's account (7), yet he modifies it in order to bring out the positive, salvific side (seen in Noah and Lot), as well as the dark, punitive side of God's activity. The heavy emphasis on water and fire as agents of judgement are there because 2 Peter will return to these images in ch. 3, and in that context both fire and water destroy in order to give birth to a new order of divine creation.

More evident, too, than in Jude is 2 Peter's pastoral call to 'rescue the godly from trial' (2. 9), a concern which will surface again in 3. 14.

CHRIST, LORD AND SAVIOUR

The Christology of 2 Peter lies somewhat in the shadow of the characteristic of God as creator and judge. Christ's role is not stated independently of the Father, but is strangely muted – a trait which some like E. Käsemann have noted as indicating a transmutation of the pristine kerygma where Christ crucified and risen is central. Yet there are some notable features.

High honours are ascribed to Jesus Christ. In a disputed text (1. 1) 'our God and Saviour Jesus Christ' (NRSV) seems to bracket two designations God/Saviour as belonging to Jesus, and, if this is so, it would be one of the rare instances where he is probably called God (the other references in the NT are Tit. 2. 13; 1 Jn. 5. 20; Rom. 9. 5; 2 Thess. 1. 12; cf. Heb. 1. 8; these are all texts open to other interpretations). Other scholars think that God and Saviour in 2 Pet. 1. 1 refer to two separate divine persons, chiefly because in 1. 2 he does make the distinction and elsewhere in the letter his favourite title is 'our Lord and Saviour Jesus Christ' (1. 11; 3. 18; cf. 2. 20; 3. 2).

'Lord' and 'Saviour' bring together two titles of unequal prominence in the NT. 'Lord' is by far the most frequent and important, and indicates Christ's risen authority and right to rule the lives of his people and the cosmos. 'Saviour', on the other hand, is only rarely attested. The references in the Pauline letters are adjectival, 'as a deliverer' (Phil. 3. 21; cf. Eph. 5. 23) and the same adjunctive or descriptive sense is found in Luke 2. 11; John 4. 42 as well as Acts 5. 31; 13. 23. As a distinct title, '*the* Saviour', the word belongs exclusively to the Pastorals (2 Tim. 1. 10; Tit. 1. 4; 2. 13; 3. 6) and is present five times in our letter (1. 1, 11; 2. 20; 3. 2, 18). It gained in currency in the Apostolic fathers, and from the mid-second century CE it became common.

'Saviour' is a quality true of Israel's God (especially Isa. 40–55), but it is likely that 2 Peter's use is drawn from the prevailing Caesar cult and/or Hellenistic saviour-gods in the mysteries. 2 Peter, then, is placing the term in prominence as a counter-thrust to the claims of his Greek environment and asserting that for Christians there is only one God and one Saviour and Lord.

Little is remarked of the gospel tradition of Jesus' life and death except the important datum of the Lord's holy commandment (2. 21; 3. 2) codified now in the apostles' testimony and the exemplary instance of the Transfiguration story (1. 16–18) of the Synoptic Gospels (Mark 9. 2–8 par.). The main reason for its introduction here lies in (i) the need to refute dependence on 'myths' by appealing to eyewitness testimony (1. 16) and (ii) the collocation of 'power and parousia' (1. 16) which paves the way for the debate over the non-arrival of the parousia in 3. 1–4, 12. The connection is made by most commentators that it is the Lord's future coming in glory, adumbrated at the Transfiguration on the Mount, that is Peter's point, though Spicq[27] argues for parousia in 1. 16 as referring to the incarnational coming of Christ of which Peter

---

[27] C. Spicq, *Les épîtres de saint Pierre*, SB Paris, 1966, 220.

and the other apostles were reliable eyewitnesses. Perhaps there is a way to combine the two dimensions and see 'powerful parousia' (a hendiadys in 1. 16) as a means of legitimating the apostolic testimony to which 2 Peter bears record. Peter's seeing the vision and hearing the heavenly voice are then the hallmarks of his authority now committed to his group and used in debate with those who evidently claimed access to superior knowledge and privilege. 2 Peter goes back to the fountain-head – to Jesus Christ who himself 'received' divine attestation (1. 17) from the Father, with the inference that the same 'holy word' authority now is conveyed to Peter's followers (as in 3. 2, and by contrast 2. 21: waverers turn back from the holy commandment that was *passed on* to them).

Christ's kingdom is both present (1. 11) and to come at the parousia of the Lord's Day (3. 12) which believers both await and hasten by their faithful living (3. 14). The 'beloved' address in 3. 14 answers to the endearing terms of the heavenly voice, 'This is my Son, the Beloved' (1. 17), the latter title having links with a Son-of-God Christology which in turn points us to the resurrection of Jesus (Acts 13. 32–4; Rom. 1. 3–4). But, if 2 Peter has a Christology at all, it is undeveloped and inchoate. Käsemann finds this to be a grave weakness; Neyrey counters that 2 Peter's concern is theological, not Christological,[28] and that within the limits of his theodicy (to explain the divine delay in retribution) the emphasis needs to fall on God, with Christ's role necessarily undeveloped.

AUTHORITY AND CHRISTIAN LIVING

2 Peter builds its case on the authority emanating from the Lord (1. 17) and transmitted to the church in the medium of prophetic scripture (1. 19–21; 3. 2, 15–17). These verses contain some of the clearest illustrations of how a community like the leaders behind 2 Peter met and responded to the threat of deviance and what they considered 'error' (2. 15–16). The example of Balaam is more elaborate than in Jude, and draws

---

[28] Neyrey, 'Form and Background', *JBL* 99/3 (1980) 430–1.

out not simply the (false) prophet's avarice, but the notice in Numbers 22. 22–35 of the donkey's rebuke of Balaam's madness. The key lies in the odd argument that Balaam was deaf to divine commands until Yahweh opened the beast's mouth and made it speak. Before then, Balaam was in need of rebuke for '*his own* transgression' – an adjective (Gr. *idios*) that Fuchs draws attention to[29] (found seven times in 2 Pet. and in five instances it related to the self-willed obstinacy of the false teachers). The opponents like Balaam were content to follow their own devices – in teaching as in interpreting scripture, both prophetic (1. 20) and Pauline (3. 16). 2 Peter's response shifts the ground to the authoritative apostolic 'word' which (correctly, the author believed) interprets prophetic oracles of judgement and claims divine sanction for it (1. 21; it is from the Holy Spirit). Also it pays due respect to Paul as a teacher of wisdom with whom the Petrine group is in accord (3. 15).

Armed with such august authority, the author sets forth in his opening section (1. 3–11) the ethical qualities that mark out the true people of God. The pericope is full of rich terminology, a lot of which is drawn from Hellenistic vocabulary and idiom ('divine power', 'divine nature', 'escape the corruption that is in the world': see earlier p. 150), but equally it has a strong Semitic flavour ('knowledge' of God need not be anything different from the OT prophetic expectation that in the last days all God's people will 'know' him, Jer. 31. 31–4; and experience his favour as they respond in obedience, Jer. 9. 23–4). The charge of moralism that is often brought against this depiction of the Christian life, along with the allegation that

the expression 'partakers of the divine nature' seems to suggest the non-eschatological understanding of redemption also espoused by Gnosticism. Instead of the primitive expectation of future consummation we now find present participation in the divine nature and its powers, i.e. deification[30]

needs some close inspection. Alongside the verdict rendered we

---

[29] E. Fuchs, *La deuxième épître*, 97.
[30] H. Koester, *Theological Dictionary of the New Testament* 9, 275.

may want to set the stress on 'faith' and 'love' as response, the list of virtues which has parallels in Pauline Christianity (Gal. 5. 22–4) as well as the deutero-Pauline Pastoral epistles (1 Tim. 6. 11; 2 Tim. 2. 22), and the way in which Koester (above) concedes that, even if 2 Peter took over a gnostic term, 'he tried to work it into his new formulation of future expectation', just as he adopted the early Christian eschatology to use as a weapon against the heretics. 'Corruption' is another case in point, since it was evidently a term coined in debate (2. 19) and maybe was placed in prominence in the paraenetic section (1. 4) to promise the antidote to the rival claims.

The practical tenor of 1. 3–11 comes through at every turn: the Christian life is a response to strenuous (1. 5: 'make every effort') and stringent (1. 9) demands. But the requirements are prefaced by the pledge of divine enabling (1. 3: 'given us') and it is God's intent that when Christians take seriously their 'calling and election' (1. 10) they will be fortified by his grace and brought to eternal felicity in Christ's ultimate kingdom which is their possession now (1. 11). In that state they are both warned not to desert (3. 17) and encouraged to mature (3. 18).

2 PETER AS WITNESS AND WARNING

This NT book exerts a strangely ambivalent effect on its readers. As we seek to piece together its life-setting and find clues about the dangers that moved the author to issue a testamentary tract, we may have some sympathy with his motivations. The author is a person impelled by strong convictions and unrelenting loyalty to the truth he felt to be under threat. One cannot but admire the way he struggles with language and thoughts not native to him, yet all designed to produce an effect. He calls on his readers to be alert, to remember, to follow the apostolic traditions, and so remain joined to the church. When evident success has drawn away a sizeable number of adherents (2. 2) and set up a rival clique, he can only appeal for a closing of ranks and a denouncing of error. The tender notes of pastoral solicitude in Jude are not here, yet the author's relationship with the readers still remains caring and warm.

His witness to God's moral character – in creation and judgement – is part of his legacy, and he shows some adaptability as he seeks to relate the Christian message to the Hellenistic world around him and to refute its aberrations as they encroached on the church's belief and living. His links of continuity with the past are strong, and he is not venturesome in his theologizing. Enough for 2 Peter to stay committed to the apostolic word in prophecy and practice.

At that point we may sense a danger. 2 Peter represents a Christianity that is on the road to becoming tradition-bound, authoritarian, and inward-looking. The next steps will be along the road to fossilization and fixation, with no room to change or to receive new light. 2 Peter, in our estimate, is not there, but its form of Christianity is potentially threatening and isolationist.

We may dismiss the vigorous use of invective (2. 21–2) and denunciation (2. 14) as the histrionics of debate – and yet perhaps feel that it is good that some such unfettered human emotions should be displayed in the New Testament writings. Less welcome, however, will be 2 Peter's rigidity and somewhat mechanical reaction to innovation and theological enterprise. But if all that 2 Peter says about the moral licence is taken at face value – and we cannot really be sure since this is only one side of the story – then the raising of a standard against 'pernicious errors' was needful to defend and conserve the 'way of righteousness', 'way of truth', 'way of integrity' ('straight way', 2. 15) in second or third generation Christianity, and preserve it for posterity.

Select bibliography

JAMES

COMMENTARIES

Listed below are commentaries in English that are likely to be found helpful. The classic work is that of Dibelius; although it was originally written early this century, it is still immensely worth reading, can be understood almost entirely without knowledge of Greek, and has been revised and brought up-to-date by Greeven. Nevertheless, it is dated and limited in some respects, and should not be read as the only or last word on James. Not least because of the wide divergence of views on the date and setting of James, it is advisable to use more than one commentary. Laws can be strongly recommended, but it should be noted that, although Greek is transliterated, it will be difficult to make full sense of the commentary without knowledge of Greek. For those with no Greek, Moo is quite recent and very good, while Mitton and the very much briefer commentaries by R. A. Martin, Reicke, and Sidebottom can all be recommended. Davids and R. P. Martin are both excellent; they are highly recommended, but again at least some knowledge of Greek is needed to make proper use of them. Mayor and Ropes are both commentaries primarily on the Greek text, with very full introductions and detailed linguistic discussion.

Adamson, J. B. (New International Commentary on the New Testament), Grand Rapids 1976.
Davids, P. H. (New International Greek New Testament Commentary), Grand Rapids 1982.
Dibelius, M. (rev. H. Greeven) (Hermeneia), ET Philadelphia 1976.
Laws, S. (Black's NT Commentaries), London 1980.
Martin, R. A. (Augsburg Commentary on the New Testament), Minneapolis 1982.
Martin, R. P. (Word Biblical Commentary), Waco 1988.

Mayor, J. B., 3rd edn., London, 1913.
Mitton, C. L. (Marshalls Study Library), London 1966.
Moo, D. (Tyndale NT Commentary), London/Grand Rapids 1985.
Reicke, B. (Anchor Bible), Garden City 1964.
Ropes, J. H. (International Critical Commentary), Edinburgh 1916.
Sidebottom, E. M. (New Century Bible), London 1967.

The German commentary of Dibelius is available in English, but it is worth mentioning here two further commentaries in German, those of Schlatter and Mussner, both of which are constantly stimulating and full of insight.

Mussner, F. (Herders Theologischer Kommentar zum NT), Freiburg 1964.
A. Schlatter, Stuttgart 1932.

BOOKS ON JAMES

There is a very great paucity of books on the theology of James, or on James more generally. Robertson and Rendall are both interesting, but dated. Hartin provides a useful discussion of a particular aspect of James, but is tendentious and misleading in a number of respects. Maynard-Reid's book is splendidly short, stimulating, and provocative. The only substantial work dealing with the letter and its theology as a whole is Adamson's book. It needs to be noted that Adamson sees the whole letter as written by James the brother of Jesus, and dates it very early. In these and other ways his interpretation begs questions, and the book is also very long (over 550 pages); but it is written in a quite popular and non-technical style, and for the most part is interesting and helpful. Popkes' recent book, in German, is not primarily concerned with the theology of James, but is certainly the best scholarly treatment of the issues raised by the letter as a whole.

Adamson, J. B., *James: the Man and his Message*, Grand Rapids 1989.
Hartin, P., *James and the Q Sayings of Jesus* (JSNTSS 47), Sheffield 1991.
Maynard-Reid, P. U., *Poverty and Wealth in James*, Maryknoll 1991.
Popkes, W., *Adressaten, Situation und Form des Jakobusbriefes* (Stuttgarter Bibelstudien 125/126), Stuttgart 1986.
Rendall, G. H., *The Epistle of James and Judaic Christianity*, Cambridge 1927.
Robertson, *Studies in the Epistle of James* (rev. edn.), Nashville 1958.

1 PETER

COMMENTARIES

Two older commentaries, both published originally in 1946, 1947 respectively, and later revised, mark the opening of a new interest in the letter.

E. G. Selwyn, *The First Epistle of St. Peter*, London 2nd edn., 1947; reprinted Grand Rapids 1981, is a standard work on the Greek text.

F. W. Beare, *The First Epistle of Peter*, Oxford, 3rd edn., 1970, is a slighter work, but marked by careful exegesis.

MORE RECENT COMMENTARIES

J. R. Michaels, *1 Peter* WBC 49, Waco 1988, carries forward the interest in the Greek text, is thorough in historical exegesis, and has a full bibliography.

On the English text, E. Best's *1 Peter*, New Century Bible Commentary (revised edn.) Grand Rapids 1982 is full of good, brief comments, and is up-to-date as far as the early 80s. J. N. D. Kelly, *A Commentary on the Epistles of Peter and Jude*, Black's New Testament Commentaries London/New York 1969 represents the fullest commentary on the English text and is probably the most serviceable for the general reader, student, and teacher.

A new phase of 1 Peter commentaries began with L. Goppelt, *Der erste Petrusbrief*, KEK 12/1, ed. F. Hahn, Göttingen 1978, who first took seriously the social setting of the epistle, a feature soon to be explored by several special studies:

J. H. Elliott, *A Home for the Homeless* whose sub-title says it all, 'A sociological exegesis of 1 Peter, its situation and strategy', London/Philadelphia 1981

D. L. Balch, *Let the Wives be Submissive. The Domestic Code in 1 Peter*, SBLDS 26, Chico, CA, 1981.

SEMI-POPULAR WORKS

In recent times a spate of books under this heading has appeared, signalling a renewed interest in 1 Peter once regarded as an 'exegetical stepchild' under the shadow of Paul's influence (J. H. Elliott's phrase). J. D. G. Dunn's *Unity and Diversity in the New Testament*,

London/Philadelphia 1977, section 76 showed how this rediscovery of Peter as a 'bridge-man', holding together varied theological positions in apostolic times, can be turned to good use, contributing to our awareness of New Testament Christianity as pluriform and many-faceted. Pursuing a more thematic approach and trying to find common elements running through the NT books, especially to do with 'faith' is J. Reumann's *Variety and Unity in New Testament Thought*, Oxford 1991, with interesting chapters (10, 15) on our letters.

C. E. B. Cranfield, *The First Epistle of Peter*, London 1950, is still one of the best, full of devotional, yet scholarly, comment.

W. A. Grudem, *The First Epistle of Peter*, Tyndale Commentary, Grand Rapids/Leicester 1988, is a popular treatment, but with some independent viewpoints.

P. H. Davids, *The First Epistle of Peter*, New International Commentary on the New Testament Grand Rapids 1990 is well regarded for exegetical depth and a rich bibliography, rivalling the material in *ANRW* 2/25, section 5 (in French, by E. Cothenet).

I. H. Marshall, *1 Peter* Leicester/Downers Grove 1991, is scholarly yet oriented to the general reader, with application made not normally found in non-homiletical works.

CONTINENTAL STUDIES

N. Brox, *Der erste Petrusbrief*, 3rd end. EKKNT 21 Zurich 1989 for depth of exegetical penetration.

S. Bénétreau, *La première épître de Pierre*, Vaux-sur-Seine 1984, is full of perceptive comment, utilized by E. P. Clowney, *The Message of 1 Peter*, Leicester/Downers Grove 1988, who offers a remarkably insightful help to the general reader, minister and teacher.

2 PETER AND JUDE

Second Peter along with Jude have been rather neglected parts of the New Testament and, until recently, have not drawn much attention in commentary writing and special studies. The letters are often lumped together indifferently with each other and with the more appealing 1 Peter.

Composite works by C. E. B. Cranfield, Torch, London 1960, B. Reicke, Anchor Bible, New York 1964, and E. M. Sidebottom, combining 2 Peter and Jude in the New Century Bible, London 1982, all suffer from limitation of space.

J. N. D. Kelly, *A Commentary on the Epistles of Peter and Jude*, BNTC, London/New York 1969 is more thorough on both epistles, and his readable work on 2 Peter is open to all the arguments that bear on the setting of this letter, its language problems, and the type of false teaching it opposes. Yet in depth and detail first place must go to R. J. Bauckham, *Jude-2 Peter*, WBC 50, Waco 1983, based on the Greek text, but written to ensure a wide appeal. It breaks fresh ground as to life setting and theological emphases by keeping 2 Peter and Jude apart as separate documents each arising from a different milieu, and by utilizing some recent continental and American studies, e.g. T. Fornberg, *An Early Church in a Pluralistic Society. A Study of 2 Peter*, Uppsala/Lund 1980, and J. H. Neyrey, *The Form and Background of the Polemic in 2 Peter* Yale University: unpublished dissertation 1977. Important Gnostic and Jewish finds from the Nag Hammadi library along with Jewish pseudepigraphical books are pressed into service in Bauckham's commentary and his later writings on the epistles.

Of special interest, and one to repay study, is the joint effort of E. Fuchs on 2 Peter and P. Reymond on Jude in the French series, CNT 13 b, Neuchâtel 1980, *La deuxième épître de saint Pierre; L'épître de saint Jude* which is full of excellent linguistic and theological observations.

On the literary patterns and stylistic–rhetorical structure of the two letters, D. F. Watson's *Invention, Arrangement, and Style. Rhetorical Criticism of Jude and 2 Peter* SBLDS 104, Atlanta, GA, 1988, is without rival. It has the fullest bibliography on these letters, comparable with R. J. Bauckham's contributions to *ANRW* 2/25, section 5 (1988).

Index for James

Index for Jude

Index for 1 Peter

AUTHORS

Index for 2 Peter

184

SUBJECTS